Z. F.

# THE PEACE CORPS
*Who, How, and Where*

# THE
# PEACE CORPS—
## *Who, How, and Where*

BY

CHARLES E. WINGENBACH

———◆———

*With a Foreword by*

SENATOR HUBERT H. HUMPHREY

THE JOHN DAY COMPANY
NEW YORK

Library of Congress Catalogue Card Number: 61-15389


Manufactured in the United States of America


Second Impression

*To My Mother and Father*

# ACKNOWLEDGMENTS

In doing this book, I have been helped by many people. Perhaps this is the best way to say thanks.

First, I want to thank Mary Ann Pearce, who patiently corrected and typed the manuscript. I am also grateful to her parents, Bill and Mary Pearce, and to the Clarks, McIntyres, and Pearces of Louisville, Kentucky, who showed me what true Southern hospitality is.

Among my friends, special thanks go to Earl Mazo and Roscoe Drummond, who have helped me with advice and opportunities over the past three years. I thank also Bob Donovan and the other staffers of the New York *Herald Tribune*, Washington Bureau, who have helped in many other ways.

To Steve Hess I am grateful for giving an unknown the chance for a book contract. Publisher Robert W. Hill and Agent Perry Knowlton deserve a prize for patience.

On Capitol Hill, Senator Hubert Humphrey and his hard-working assistant, Win Griffith, have been particularly helpful, as has the charming Senator Maurine Neuberger. Congressman Henry Reuss also assisted the project.

7

ACKNOWLEDGMENTS

I would like to express appreciation to Attorney General Robert Kennedy and his information aide, Jack Rosenthal. And further along Pennsylvania Avenue I thank Pierre Salinger, Harris Wofford, and Richard Goodwin of the White House staff.

There is hardly anyone on the Peace Corps staff who did not give aid beyond the call of duty, but at the top of the list are Bill Haddad, Gordon Boyce, Pat Kennedy, Sally Bowles, Mitzi Mallina, Tom Matthews, Pete Grothe, Tom Quimby and Jim Moody.

Equal gratitude goes to the private voluntary agencies. In the International Voluntary Services, Dr. J. S. Noffsinger. The American Friends Service Committee —Dr. Clarence Pickett, Steve Carey, Polly Frazier, Ed Wright, and Nancy Duryea. Catholic Relief Services— Bob Melina, Monsignor Joseph Harnett, and Mary O'Hara. And, finally, Reverend James Robinson and Richard McFarland of Crossroads Africa, Dr. Wayland Zwayer of the American Voluntary Agencies Council, and Bill Nighswonger of World Neighbors.

Thanks also to Andy Rice and Frank Land of the Colorado State University Research Foundation.

For putting up with countless requests for information, I'm grateful to Miss Adoreen McCormick and Mrs. Jeanne Burch of the Library of Congress.

# CONTENTS

## PART FOUR

### ORGANIZATION AND ADMINISTRA-<br>TION     131

## PART FIVE

### AN INTERNATIONAL PEACE CORPS?     151

# Foreword

The Peace Corps, transformed in a few quick months from dream to reality, is a practical result of President Kennedy's inaugural plea: "Let us begin."

None of us who worked to organize and develop the Peace Corps claim that it will be the final answer to the tensions and miseries of a restless world.

We do believe—deeply and confidently—that the Peace Corps is a vital step toward fulfillment of our goal.

Our goal is becoming more distinct as we witness millions of people in underdeveloped regions of the world rising against the intolerable conditions and miseries of the past. We seek a world in which mankind is relieved of the ancient enemies of freedom and the loyal allies of totalitarianism—poverty, hunger, disease and illiteracy.

The purpose of the Peace Corps is keyed to helping men and women help themselves to security, to progress, to individual dignity. The Peace Corps is not and should never be a mere propaganda gimmick or a weapon of the Cold War. It is and must remain an effective tool for peace and progress throughout the world.

11

The Peace Corps also offers a new and dramatic dimension to America's concern for the welfare of other peoples and to its efforts to help build the solid foundations for peace.

Peace is not passive; it is not merely the absence of violence. There can be no peace for the middle-aged woman in Burma suffering from malaria. There can be no peace for the emaciated teen-age boy in India who survives—barely—on several hundred calories a day. There can be no peace for the illiterate and unskilled tribesman in Tanganyika bound to a quagmire of want.

The United States today is committed to placing a man on the moon in this decade. For that exciting goal, we have a plan, a program—and a budget.

Is one man on the moon any more important than half of mankind in misery?

To lift mankind to higher levels of decency and dignity, we also need a commitment, a plan and a program.

We must offer to the underdeveloped regions of the world more than cash and high-level technical advisers. We must offer to the peoples of those lands desperately needed operational skills and the training to allow those skills to endure and multiply among local citizens.

Under our new commitment and program, we must also offer the hand of friendship. The day is gone when the United States will deal only with the governments of nations and when well-paid, well-housed American personnel deal with local "natives" as superiors.

Our efforts overseas today need a touch of humility. Our people must approach the people of other lands as equals, as partners, as fellow human beings willing to share the skills and work needed to build a better life for all.

That is the task of Peace Corps volunteers. They will not work and live in American ghettos of luxury in underdeveloped lands. They will share the joys and pains, the frustrations and hopes of the people they seek to serve.

The dream of a Peace Corps is now reality. The need now is for realistic plans to give force to the Peace Corps, and realistic understanding of the challenge to the Peace Corps and its members.

Charles Wingenbach helps provide that understanding in this book.

The American people must seek to understand both the opportunities and problems of the Peace Corps. They must reject both the mocking skepticism and the head-in-the-clouds type of optimism so often expressed for the Peace Corps.

They must be prepared for some mistakes, some failures and even some casualties as the Peace Corps develops and grows.

But more important, they must have the vision to see the magnificent potential of the Peace Corps.

The real power of the United States is not in the Government. It is not in the modern weapons of destruction or the tools of industry.

The real power of America is in the people, in the compassion of individual Americans for others and in their capacity of skills and dedication to help others.

The sooner we put that power to work in the world's zone of misery, the sooner peace will be secured.

That is the purpose of the Peace Corps. That is the goal of America. That is the hope of man.

HUBERT H. HUMPHREY

13

# INTRODUCTION

## HISTORY OF THE PEACE CORPS
## MOVEMENT

You will live in a small wooden house, sleep on the floor on a bamboo mat, with a pillow stuffed with rice grain and a mosquito net to protect you from the swarm of bloodthirsty mosquitoes. The heavy humid heat and the hard bed will not be comfortable. You will go down to the well to get water to wash your face. Make sure to boil it before drinking it to avoid malaria. . . . Soon the sun will turn extremely hot and you will be expected to work in the field in the hot sun with the other men, because only when you are ready to share in the work of the people you want to live with will you be able to be one of them.

Let us pretend that you will teach—your students will come with just a piece of chalk and a slate to no schoolhouse . . . those that don't have a slate can trace letters with their fingers in the dust. . . . In the monsoon you will suffer from the damp weather but nothing changes. . . . The work is the same, only now leeches will cling to you; worms, frogs and snakes will be numerous. The roof will probably leak and all the time you will have to eat with your fingers as other utensils are nonexistent.

Will you be able to take all this?

KHIN KHIN HLA, a Burmese student [1]

[1] New York *Herald Tribune,* March 27, 1961.

Apparently President John F. Kennedy was aware of the hardships when he set up the Peace Corps by executive order last March. Select American men and women are to journey to distant lands "to help [them] meet their urgent needs for skilled manpower." [2]

Public response, encouraged by Mr. Kennedy's appeals during the campaign last year, has been largely favorable. Students on campuses across the nation— and many of their elders—see the idea as a revolutionary concept that will reawaken America to what they consider our lost national purpose: the "task of bringing to man that decent way of life which is the foundation of freedom and a condition of peace." [3]

Skeptics are not hard to find, however, and here the issue has made some strange bedfellows. Former Vice-President Nixon called the Peace Corps "a haven for draft dodgers," and one conservative Washington columnist has ridiculed it as a Children's Crusade. Radio Moscow, meanwhile, insists that it is just a cynical front for U. S. intelligence agents to infiltrate and re-enslave the former Western colonies; the leftist Pan-Africa People's Conference has condemned the proposal on similar grounds.

## Not a New Idea

What many of the Peace Corps' supporters and critics do not realize is this: the idea is not new. It is more than a century old at least, and some traces of it could probably be found in the missions Alexander the Great sent to the Orient. What is more, it has been tried—with varying degrees of success *and* failure

[2] From the statement accompanying the executive order, March 1, 1961.
[3] *Ibid.*

—by governments and private agencies in recent times.

In 1850, British writers Thomas Carlyle and John Ruskin advocated "industrial regiments . . . to fight the bogs and wildernesses at home and abroad. . . ." [4] Ruskin attempted to implement the idea by having Oxford dons and students build a road nearby, but it was a dismal flop.

The Old World was crumbling, and the United States, under the first Roosevelt, had temporarily emerged from isolation when, in 1904, philosopher William James proposed to the Universal Peace Congress in Boston that draft-age young men be put to work building, not destroying. James called his project "the moral equivalent of war," and said that the newly directed discipline would produce "toughness without callousness, authority with as little criminal cruelty as possible, and painful work done cheerily because the duty is temporary, and threatens not, as now, to degrade the whole remainder of one's life." [5]

He and his contemporaries had seen the example of the Spanish-American War veterans who stayed behind in the Philippines to teach and work in the barrios. But they realized some of their wildest hopes when, a generation later, President Franklin D. Roosevelt inaugurated his three-pronged youth resources effort: the Civilian Conservation Corps (CCC), the Work Projects Administration (WPA), and the National Youth Administration (NYA). These emergency work-relief and vocational training programs snowballed because, in the depression economy of the early

[4] Thomas Carlyle, *Latter-Day Pamphlets* (New York: Harper, 1850), pp. 42–43.
[5] William James, *Memories and Studies* (New York: Longmans, 1912), pp. 290–291.

thirties, nearly 14 million workers were unemployed, and approximately 30 per cent of these were youths between the ages of sixteen and twenty-four. A "vicious circle" worked against national recovery—young men could not obtain jobs to learn skills, yet employers refused to hire anyone without skill and experience. Work camps were set up, and the unskilled did everything from planting tree seedlings to constructing bridges and dams.

How useful this was in practical terms will probably be debated for years to come. But many CCC veterans, ranging in occupation from a Minnesota congressman to a Vermont truck driver, say that it gave real purpose and work to jobless men who might otherwise have degenerated into the same sort of restless mobs that catapulted Hitler to power during those same years.

Programs of this nature were necessarily temporary and limited in scope. Churches and private voluntary agencies had been working in the field long before the Great Depression forced the United States and several European countries to enlist the services of their youthful citizens. National recovery, though, formed only a small part of their agenda. In addition, financed by private contributions and government grants, their projects have sent thousands of men and women abroad to instruct illiterate peasants in sanitation and the three R's, better ways to farm and to conserve natural resources, and now perform a hundred other community services as well.

## How the Project Began

The embryo existed in the work of the private agencies, but Project Peace Corps is the child both of chance and of hard work by its never-say-die supporters. Exactly how or when it was born, no one knows.

In 1954, Heinz Rollman, a North Carolina industrialist and wartime refugee from Hitler's Germany, wrote a book titled *World Construction*, which he mailed to government officials and opinion makers throughout the free world. His principal proposals were a 3-million-man "Peace Army" of draftees to work in underdeveloped nations and an increase of foreign exchange students to five million. During the 1960 political campaign, President Eisenhower derided Democrat Kennedy's Peace Corps as a warmed-over version of ideas originated by Heinz Rollman, at the time a Republican candidate for Congress.

Little else was heard of the idea for the next couple of years after the distribution of Mr. Rollman's book. In 1957, a group of Congressmen visited the Southeast Asian nation of Cambodia to see how U. S. taxpayers' money was being used in the foreign aid program.

One day they drove for miles along a new modern highway without spotting a single motorist. A solitary farmer trudged down the edge of the deserted road, his water buffalo in tow. Yet $30 million in American aid, plus valuable time and technical know-how, had been poured into the project.

Further on, however, they came to a village in the jungle. An elementary school stood in the clearing, and four young Americans told the visiting dignitaries how they had built it with primitive tools and manual labor. Just a short time before, the four had been schoolteachers back in the States; now they were going from village to village, teaching an Asian people how to read and write.

19

Their example set one member of the party, Representative Henry S. Reuss of Wisconsin, to thinking how the $30 million spent on the highway might better have been used to finance the work of thousands like them. Later, at Cornell University, he expanded the idea into a proposal for a Point 4 youth corps. The students were so enthusiastic that thereafter he buttonholed everyone who would listen to him about it.

However, he was not the only prominent figure thinking along these lines. The Peace Corps' present Director, R. Sargent Shriver, then a Chicago educator and one-time leader of the Experiment in International Living, returned that same year from a swing through Asia to present a similar idea to President Eisenhower as an extension of the Administration's People-to-People program, but nothing came of it.

Meanwhile, Dr. Tom Dooley's work in Laos had begun to generate a lot of public interest. By late 1959, the situation had jelled sufficiently for Congressman Reuss to introduce legislation in the House for a study of the proposal; the late Senator Richard L. Neuberger of Oregon introduced a companion measure in the Senate.

The wind was almost knocked out of the project even before it began. When the Reuss bill came up before the House Appropriations Committee, Chairman Otto Passman of Louisiana, a perennial foreign aid foe, struck out the $10,000 budget for the study. Peace Corps supporters were dismayed, but Reuss went to work at once on Passman, who finally gave in and agreed that if the Senate restored the money, he would go along with the joint conference. Senator Hubert H. Humphrey of Minnesota sent an urgent plea to the Senate Appropriations Committee chairman, Carl Hayden of Arizona, and the funds were put back in the bill. Congress authorized the study in June, 1960, and that November the International Co-operation Administration (ICA) farmed out the contract to Colorado State University.

Senator Humphrey was an early backer of the Corps. Impressed by the success of the Quakers (American Friends Service Committee), he had tested its appeal before college groups on several occasions in 1957. The time came, however, when he tired of reading studies and longed instead for action. In the spring of 1960, the Senator detailed a foreign relations adviser, Peter Grothe, to see whether the project was actually feasible enough to start work on it right away. Grothe spent six weeks interviewing private agency workers and digging through available material, and he also got an unexpected assist from two Yale and Harvard graduate students who had been unaware of the Reuss efforts.

In his final report, young Grothe conservatively estimated that 10,000 volunteers could be sent into the field within four or five years; the Senator, often accused of radical leanings, slashed this down still further to 5,000 on a trial basis. Then on June 16, he formally proposed to the Senate that a U. S. Peace Corps be set up immediately. A deluge of favorable mail poured in, dwarfing both the U-2 incident and Fidel Castro in interest.

How and when did John F. Kennedy decide to adopt the proposal? Many of his aids insist that it was a fluke, but the evidence indicates that it was deliberately timed for maximum political appeal. Several in the Americans for Democratic Action (A.D.A.) wing of the party have said that after battling Senator

Humphrey's grip on Democratic liberals, Kennedy thought that the idealism of the Peace Corps could help swing still-reluctant Stevensonians and perhaps a Rockefeller Republican or two into his camp. The New Frontier hopeful probably also remembered how the New Deal's Franklin D. Roosevelt capitalized on the CCC in his own first Presidential race.

In February, Kennedy faced his first question on the Corps while appearing on the New York television program, *College News Conference*. He admitted that he didn't know much about it, but when he returned to Washington, he instructed his staff to work on the idea.

The next link in the chain of events was seven months later. In September, after Kennedy had won the nomination, Peter Grothe took the Humphrey proposal to Archibald Cox, at the time the candidate's chief speech writer and now the U. S. Solicitor-General. Advisers in the Kennedy brain trust had already pointed out the idea's potential, both as a new foreign policy breakthrough and as an election issue, and the Humphrey "Youth Peace Corps" was incorporated into certain future papers on the subject by Kennedy's advisers.

Chester Bowles, a one-time liberal dark-horse candidate and now Under Secretary of State, discussed the Peace Corps with Kennedy and made several campaign speeches about it. Sam and Nancy Bowles, his son and daughter-in-law, are in Nigeria as teachers.

Once made, the proposal caught like wildfire—and under the most unlikely circumstances. It was a tired and dispirited Kennedy campaign crew that, having arrived on the campus long after midnight on October

14, 1960, listened as their chief asked 10,000 University of Michigan students to give as much as ten years of their lives to serving mankind. The audience responded with an ovation, and despite the early hour some hardy souls began forming on the spot committees to push the project.

Barnstorming from city to city, Kennedy let the issue simmer a while and went on to other topics. However, both he and his opponent met more than an occasional question on the Peace Corps, although newspaper coverage of the Michigan speech was meager. And, in late October, Army General James M. Gavin, now U. S. Ambassador to France, spoke of the idea to the Nuclear Energy Regional Advisory Council in Miami, and then took it up with the Democratic candidate.

Kennedy's timing reportedly caught the Nixon camp off base. The Vice-President's unenthusiastic treatment of such ideas disgruntled many Rockefeller Republicans who still considered the liberal Governor of New York their party's best bet. An adviser on African affairs testifies that in the early stages of the campaign he gave Nixon a study outlining a youth corps, but, as it turned out later, the plan was shelved. In the meantime Robert Bowie, policy planning chief under the late Secretary of State Dulles, urged a Senate subcommittee to enlist 1,000 college graduates a year in a Foreign Service junior technical assistance corps; later President Eisenhower's Committee on Information Activities Abroad suggested a similar long-term overseas youth aid program. A close aide to the former President said that the proposal was brought up at White House conferences and vetoed, mainly on objections from the Pentagon; he added, however, that

23

both Eisenhower and Nixon spiritually liked the concept, but the grave reservations they had for its success overruled their sympathies.

Ironically, rumors of an impending Nixon proposal of a youth aid program are said to have spurred Kennedy's headline-making speech November 2nd in San Francisco. But to this day Nixon vehemently denies that he ever had any intentions of the kind. Nor will the new President's staff officially admit any more than mere coincidence in his choice of Nixon's home state for the project's formal launching.

The San Francisco speech was written by Theodore (Ted) Sorenson—then and now Kennedy's right-hand man—and Richard Goodwin, a White House expert on Latin America. Kennedy broadened the Humphrey-Reuss concept to include women and older persons, and he also offered a draft exemption to volunteers. This last caused him no end of trouble and earned Nixon's scorn for the proposal.

The choice of the name "Peace Corps" indicates an uncertainty in Kennedy's mind as to the scope of the project. He gave it that title in San Francisco, but as late as last January the President-elect's headquarters in New York called it the "International Youth Service Agency," the name suggested by Professor Max F. Millikan of Massachusetts Institute of Technology. The present title was partly a concession to Senator Humphrey, who argued that we need to restore to the word peace the true meaning Communist jargon has stolen from it. And it shows Kennedy's return to his original stand that the Peace Corps should have no arbitrary age limits.

For a time after the election, little was heard of the Peace Corps. Compared with the delicate tasks of choosing cabinet officers and smoothing the transition from the old regime to the new, the project was relatively low on the priority list of things that had to be done.

Nevertheless, a minor miracle of organization took place. Sargent Shriver and Harris Wofford, who is now the White House liaison with the Peace Corps, were given the job of making and co-ordinating plans for the new agency. Before half of the first Hundred Days was up, the President had created it by executive fiat. For such a controversial program, this was bold by anyone's standards. The awesome F.D.R. had waited for Congress to authorize the CCC; Kennedy first gave the order and later asked the jealous solons to approve it. It was reasoned that, to avoid red tape and to give it the greatest impact, this was the only course if the program was ever to get underway. But the new Chief Executive recognized the political hazards involved and tried to get former Republican President Herbert Hoover to act as the program's chairman. When Hoover gingerly declined for equally political reasons, Vice-President Lyndon B. Johnson, a past master in handling Capitol Hill, was named to head an advisory council drawn from many professional walks of life.

## The Future

Now that the Peace Corps is off the ground, many questions about it come to mind. What are its prospects? What will be its role at home and abroad? What dangers and requirements lie in the way of success?

Most important, what sort of people will be recruited? What will be their training? Experienced missionaries and businessmen fear that the popular new government agency, eager to confound its critics, will send relatively untrained, comfort-conscious youths to touchy new nations as shirt-sleeve ambassadors. Are these fears justified? Can these "kids" accomplish something that has baffled veteran diplomats —namely, how to get through to the hearts and minds of the world's non-white majority.

For these questions, there is no better answer than the vast experience of the private voluntary agencies. They have come up against the same obstacles, and what they have learned will probably set the guidelines for the Peace Corps.

No attempt is made in this book to persuade anyone to join or support the Peace Corps. What *is* attempted is a frank appraisal of the promise and the perils confronting it. How far the new government agency will match or surpass the work of private volunteers is, at this point, anyone's guess.

CHARLES E. WINGENBACH

# PART ONE

# TRIAL AND ERROR:

# THE NEED AND THE

# EXPERIENCE

The young doctor studies a sickly child. He turns to the mother, and says, "The boy has malaria. But a few injections, good sleep and patient care, and he'll be out with his playmates in no time. Be sure to bring him back tomorrow, señora." The Indian girl nods in understanding, but watching her leave, the doctor knows he has won only half the battle.

She takes the child into the waiting room, where the ancient grandmother greets her grimly. But they are silent as they walk home.

As they stoop to enter the airless adobe hut, the old woman's voice breaks out in scorn. "The white man has fed you a lot of tales. But you believed him and his mission padres. Would you take the cloves and goat's milk to the hag of the hill? No, you think it is superstitious and unscientific! Ha, what does science know of the evil powers of the witch? In revenge she has put Juanito on his deathbed. The foreigner can do nothing for him, no matter what he says. Will you still defy all the traditions of our ancestors? Must your child and our whole village be cursed so that we will have no rest after we die? Come, we will go and promise the hag we will not take Juanito to the hospital."

Finally, the terror-stricken young widow gives in, and the two leave to pay tribute to the unknown.

Two days later, Juanito dies. It is God's will.

Thousands like Juanito die every day, and superstition is but one of the reasons why. And, like the young doctor, many would-be Samaritans have lent elbow grease and know-how only to find their efforts stymied at every turn. Not a few have wondered if the effort is really worth while.

Perhaps it is the "fellowship of pain" that Tom Dooley often spoke of in trying to explain why he sacrificed a brilliant career in order to heal the penniless sick of Asian jungles. Or perhaps it is to spread the benefits of modern industry and agriculture to an awakening African continent which still uses the technology of medieval Europe. Whatever the reason, private American citizens have considered this work so important that, since 1939, they have contributed over $3 billion to voluntary agencies providing such aid to about 100 nations.

As if this were not enough, the Kennedy Administration has recently established the Peace Corps. Its objective is "work assistance" at the grass-roots level. For the most part, Corpsmen will be volunteers fresh out of college, not seasoned diplomats or technical experts. The Point 4 concept was a new and revolutionary chapter in American foreign policy. Even more so is a government-sponsored Peace Corps.

However, there is nothing new in the use of semiskilled youth for overseas assistance. The Quakers (American Friends Service Committee) started their program even before the coals of World War I had had a chance to cool. And in 1960 the UNESCO Coordination Committee listed 133 work camps in 32 countries, with 80 different organizations as patrons.

Experience in the field is vast, but so is the need. The idea that top-level programming is the cure-all for the world's ills is as outdated as Henry Ford's Model T. In 1953 Dr. Mottram P. Torre, consultant to the Mutual Security Agency, gave this testimony: "The few failures due to the lack of technical competence were related to a person with the wrong kind of skills being recruited to do the job rather than a person who lacked technical competence. *Many of the men were overqualified and had skills far beyond the need of the immediate situation. . . .*" [1] The moral is that villages still at the fifteenth century level have little use for the highly mechanized skills of the Atomic Age. The voluntary agencies have pioneered in filling the more practical needs.

The purposes of a Peace Corps type of operation are many and varied. The basic one, though, is "institution building." The Western tradition of voluntary service is foreign to many cultures, and a developing nation lacking it is hard put to erect the necessary framework for a healthy political, economic and social life. Example by actual physical co-operation in self-help can, therefore, be very valuable since it does not smack of the patronizing condescension that so often accompanies foreign aid. Concretely, this means that an educated young citizen of a foreign nation working alongside his peer from America will acquire

[1] *The Administration of Technical Assistance: Growth in the Americas,* by Philip M. Glick (Chicago: University of Chicago Press, 1957), p. 146.

enough respect for honest sweat and toil to build up functioning private and government organisms, instead of mass bureaucracies.

A successful private agency doing just this is the International Voluntary Services. Since 1953, IVS has sent over 200 youths as junior technicians to Africa, Indochina and the Near East. Most of its volunteers grew up on family farms and bring practical skills to their work. These young men are used to tinkering around with engines, repairing tools, using simple carpentry to fix up an old barn and other rudimentary techniques that aren't ordinarily acquired through formal schooling. However, all IVS team members must be college graduates, and they must tackle a variety of tasks ranging from animal husbandry to rigging a makeshift well.

There is no room, on the other hand, for mass projects like leaf raking, ditch digging or the like which seem to fascinate those who see the Peace Corps as a glorified overseas CCC. The new nations have more than enough unemployed laborers who can be used for these purposes, and the surest way to scuttle the new foreign aid concept would be to send droves of eager, adventure-seeking youths to add to this pool. Even in the Peace Corps there are some who view it first and foremost as cultural exchange, and only incidentally as a hardheaded humanitarian effort to help the Nigerian or the Indonesian to raise his standard of living and gain effectiveness in new techniques. If the private agencies have learned anything, it is that people who are trying to pull themselves up by their bootstraps have only contempt for that sort of naïveté. Moreover, they would have good reason to suspect the motives behind any large-scale invasion

by foreigners who mouth idealism but offer no practical solutions to their problems.

This last point is important. IVS and other groups
have found it best not to assign more than five or ten
Americans to any one project, and these must be
matched by local "counterparts" or work associates.
For example, an American public health volunteer
in Laos would work side by side with a *medecin in-
dochinois,* who may have the equivalent of grade
school education plus a smattering of medical know-
how. The Laotian learns by doing, and the American
gets an understanding of the average villager's special
needs and quirks, and vice versa. No amount of mere
cultural exchange could accomplish that.

## The Communist Challenge

Another category of well-wisher is the "crusader."
Whether right or left, he wants to use the Peace Corps
as a new U. S. propaganda arm. The conservative
argues something like this: "Since the taxpayer is foot-
ing the bill, our boys and girls should sell our American free-enterprise system abroad." For the left, it's "a
bold new program to counter Russian advances in
the underdeveloped countries of the world."

But, as Al Smith once said, no matter how you
slice it, it's still baloney. Either approach would mean
the kiss of death for the Peace Corps in neutralist
Africa and Asia or even allied Latin America. No
foreign politician sensitive to the public pulse would
dare welcome Americans under such a guise.

On the other hand, the Cold War *does* exist. It is
obvious that success in aid projects will inevitably
benefit the foreign policy of the bloc sponsoring them.
An African aid advisor to Khrushchev, Professor I. I.

Potekhin, frankly admitted Russia's propaganda aims. "One of our major tasks," he said, "[is] to establish the truth about Africa—not because we want it, but because we want to help the Africans understand their history better." American reporter Marvin Kalb asked him if this meant in terms of Marxism-Leninism. "There is no other truth," Potekhin replied. "And I can assure you that no one working in this institute has any other truth." [2]

No better showcase for Soviet bloc assistance exists than the former French-African colony of Guinea. Yet, when the Guinean government asked the Eisenhower Administration for technical assistance and loans, they got a cold shoulder. The reasons were obvious: when France saw that Guinea would not toe the line, she withdrew all her civil servants at once and the African nation teetered on total collapse. The United States, anxious not to displease her proud ally, went along in everything, and Guinea, spurned, turned to the East.

Reverend William Coffin, Yale University chaplain and Peace Corps advisor, headed a work-camp project last year in Guinea for Operation Crossroads-Africa. This is the account he gave of his experience:

"We Crossroaders were practically the first Americans in Guinea. Sekou Toure welcomed us, as he and his people are anxious to reverse what they regard as a hostile American press.

"Communist technicians are everywhere. The Russians said they had twelve teachers in secondary schools, but I only met three of them. Since I speak Russian, I got to know them fairly well. None were

[2] "Russia's Own 'Peace Corps' for Africa," *The Reporter*, April 13, 1961.

over twenty-three, but strangely they were ill at ease with Guineans, which is remarkable considering the favor they enjoy there.

"The Red propaganda effort is at the point of saturation. Radio Peking beams loud and clear, and only regional stations can be heard better. You can hear Voice of America, but not too well. The book-stores in Conakry are filled with slick, readable Soviet bloc magazines, and I saw an East German 'White Paper' on Western imperialism.

"People ask why is Guinea important, why Guineans are hostile to our country. The answer is Guineans do not think in Cold War terms of East and West. For them, it's North and South. North is white European colonialism, and South is black Africa. Perhaps because they have had no adverse involvement with Communism, Guineans cannot understand what the Cold War means.

"We Americans have too often asked too much of Guinea, and given too little. The U.S.A. has been regarded as overloyal to her European colonial allies. Neither have our earlier feelers toward Guinea been any more judicious. When we finally got around to recognizing that Guinea exists, the International Co-operation Administration (ICA) demanded full diplomatic immunity for all our technicians. The Russians and Chinese had asked no favors, so Toure angrily refused.

"Jim Crow is the worst albatross around our neck, and it's kind of embarrassing when we have to wear it and try to talk to Africa at the same time. Twice I realized just what this means—once as a white American in Guinea, and later when I was jailed with other Freedom Riders in Montgomery.

"Any Peace Corpsman who goes to Guinea will have to know what he's talking about. He should know Marxist dialectics and have a thorough background in the issues behind the news. This means segregation in our country as well as the history of Russian vetoes in the UN. He must not attempt to proselytize, but there will be questions and he should be prepared to answer them."

Both President Kennedy and Director Shriver have stressed over and over again the humanitarian emphasis of the Peace Corps, and the private agencies know from long experience that no other objective can succeed. But, as Reverend Coffin suggested, American representatives cannot forever turn the other cheek when quizzed by curious neutralists or professional agitators. Otherwise, they will lose face; in face-conscious countries, that would be just as fatal as blatant propaganda.

American Friends Service Committee official Stephen Carey agrees that it is a delicate task, but he thinks that the quiet example of unselfish work will, in the long run, be more valuable than any amount of persuasion. Numerous cases can be cited to back up his claim. At the time the Suez crisis exploded in 1956, an IVS team of two was working an experimental farm in Egypt. The villagers stood in long queues to see them off, and Moslem fathers who had worked with them in the fields paid the young Americans unusual tribute by naming their children after them. After the Suez conflict was over, President Gamal Abdel Nasser asked IVS to send the two back, along with ten more like them. The first Crossroads group had a similar experience. When they arrived at an airport in West Africa the air was heavy with suspicion. One young African would help with the luggage of his Negro guests only; when he found he had been carrying a white girl's suitcase, he tossed it across the ground. Luckily, American tempers were held in check and an even more unpleasant incident was avoided. In three weeks, however, whites and blacks were working together, and the African apologized to the girl.

## Terrors on the Domestic Front

Foreign-aid workers readily admit that while they will gladly take on any number or size of difficulties abroad, they quail at the thought of the twin terrors back home: government red tape and the Congressional appropriations system. Many good ideas start in the flush of idealism and courage, only to be ground between the two and emerge as faceless, expensive and repetitive bureaucracies. For that reason, the private agencies are reluctant to surrender their independence; one spokesman expressed the fear that the Peace Corps will swallow up its parents and become a "junior ICA."

Most red tape stems from the awkward system of Congressional appropriations for government projects. The routine seems deceptively necessary and logical, even simple on the face of it. But a new agency inherits the procedures, good and bad, of its predecessor, as well as a welter of confusing advice from the whole federal structure. In Washington, the agency receives reports and estimates from the field, plus private estimates of needed projects by the host government. In turn it has to anticipate difficulties by trying to determine in advance just how much it can allocate to each sector. Then the statistics must pass through the sensitive fingers of the Budget Bureau and under the politically minded eyes of the members of Congress. More often than not, Congress sharply reduces funds, and may even begin the whole rigmarole of questioning whether the agency is necessary after all. Or a Congressman may add a pet project or two, while cutting the money for another project which an involved consultation between field chiefs, the host government, interagency conferees and dozens of others had already judged imperative. As one wag remarked, it is usually for "reasons known only to God and the constituents back in Podunk."

Harlan Cleveland, the present Assistant Secretary of State for International Organization Affairs, summed up the problem neatly: "We know in our hearts that we are in the world for keeps, yet we are still tackling twenty-year problems with five-year plans staffed with two-year personnel working with one-year appropriations." A former ICA project chief differed with this judgment in only one respect, namely that today's problems will take far longer than twenty years to solve.

The situation may improve, however, with both a sympathetic President and sympathetic Congressional leaders in the saddle. But even this is no guarantee. When he first recommended the Marshall Plan, President Harry Truman asked for long-term appropriations. Congress judged that his request would unduly curtail the powers of review which it so jealously guards, and the present one-year system was retained.

## Specific Needs

Why, despite certain misgivings about domestic and foreign obstacles, do most voluntary agencies insist that the Peace Corps is necessary? Just how necessary is it?

Half the world is in poverty, hunger and disease. Over two thirds of the people of Africa, Asia, and Latin America are illiterate. As Senator Humphrey told Congress last year, no nation can compete in this highly competitive world without a literate population. In fact, though, many social scientists agree that a concerted effort could wipe out a substantial number of so-called population problems. The rich nations continue to get richer, but the poorer nations become still poorer daily. Someone once remarked that only when one has encountered the smell of death, the paralysis of despair, and the passions of frustrations working among a whole people that the total physical reality of the problem comes home to him.

The peoples of these nations do not, and will not, stand still. Colonialism is fading away, but the problems arising in its place make it seem to pale by comparison. Lack of an adequate elite is pushing the emerging nations to their limit; if not remedied, extremist solutions will find favor and nations that could have formed a buffer third force will end up as mere pawns of the two giant blocs. It may seem cliché ridden to say that world peace itself is at stake, but the evidence provided by the Congo and Cuba shows it to be nothing more than the truth.

The human tragedy is worst of all. In one area of Taiwan alone, 80 per cent of the population—men, women and children—were found to be afflicted with crippling goiters. Simple medical techniques and early care could prevent or reduce the disease. In another region, the Catholic Relief Services came across thousands of peasant families who lacked even the simplest of bedding for the damp monsoon season. All that was required was a cotton-processing machine to make "footans," a five-pound cotton quilt. These do-it-your-self methods preserved the health of the people and released part of their meager resources for other family necessities.

The urgency of the need has been underscored by the Peace Corps' reception in underdeveloped countries. Speaking of his world tour last June, Director Shriver told an audience at De Paul University:

"Prime Minister Nehru asked us for agricultural extension workers to help meet India's staggering food deficiency. Gandhi himself had said India teems with millions who have to go *without* two meals a day and to whom the only form in which God dare appear is food. . . .

Prime Minister Nkrumah of Ghana asked for plumbers, teachers, and electricians. 'Send us teachers,' he said, 'teachers of science and math and of all subjects—teachers for our elementary schools and our secondary schools and our universities. And send them,' he asked, 'by August!'

U Nu in Burma wants health workers—sanitation engineers, nurses and nurses' aids, doctors, dental technicians, just to mention a few—and he needs them desperately to help his people lift the burden of disease from their lives.

The leaders of Nigeria—Prime Minister Azikiwe, Sir Tafewa Balewa, and Sardona of Sukutu—unanimously requested teachers. A similar request came from President Garcias of the Philippines . . . [who] has asked the Peace Corps—and we have agreed—to send 300 *teachers' aids* to stem the current deterioration of English instruction. . . ."

40

Earlier, it had been announced that Corpsmen would work in Tanganyika as surveyors, geologists and civil engineers to help native technicians map and construct roads, and CARE has contracted with the Peace Corps to carry out a community development project in Colombia.

The problems are immense when viewed as a whole. But efforts on an individual, grass-roots level have been undertaken, and some of the more pressing hardships have been relieved. It goes to say, therefore, that while greater resources is not the only solution, it certainly must be regarded as a principal one. The private agencies simply have not got and cannot supply by themselves what is needed, and the vast ability of the Federal Government to enlist adequate funds and trained personnel would seem the only answer. Indeed, it might even be practical to extend the effort beyond the private and the national levels to that of the United Nations. But, for the present, that is mere speculation. What the voluntary people *are* certain of is that a U. S. Peace Corps must be put on a permanent, expanding basis.

# PART TWO

---

# THE GREAT BOTTLENECK:

# SELECTION

# AND TRAINING

# CHAPTER 1

# WHO SHOULD SERVE?

Of all the tasks an organization has to tackle, the most difficult is recruiting the right people for the job. One misfit can undo years of painful planning and hard work.

This is especially true in selecting workers for service overseas. Faults that one's own countrymen might overlook become inexcusable among a sensitive foreign people. Eugene Burdick's *The Ugly American* was, if anything, an understatement of the dangers in this area. Consequently, regardless of how costly and involved an adequate process of rigid screening and selection may be, experts in the field—government and private enterprise alike—feel this is one place where cost must be ignored. The future of the Peace Corps will depend primarily on the success or failure of the first teams sent abroad.

The need for caution is a matter of concern for the foreign aid advocate as well as its foe. The Peace Corps should not be an escape for our often-cited "restless and purposeless youth." One United Nations technician summed up his doubts with this comment: "As I see it, these bumptious kids are an American problem; can't we solve it without bothering the rest of the world?" That this fear is widespread—and to a degree justified—was testified to by Jack Gould, television critic for *The New York Times:*

> Last night's television documentary "The Red and the Black" provided a strong argument against unleashing ill-prepared youngsters on an unsuspecting world. . . . The interviews were chilling in the extreme. Though their ostensible mission was to teach, not one of the young people could claim professional teaching experience. None had familiarity with the [host] language . . . in the arena of international affairs they were practically inarticulate. . . . The youngsters, whose chief qualifications seemed to be wholesomeness, good will, and energy, inevitably invited a conclusion that the underdeveloped countries had been made the latest stop for wide-eyed American tourists.[1]

The youths Gould spoke of were in Guinea as English teachers, and his complaint was supported by the Guinean Government. Three out of twenty American teachers sent to Guinea broke their two-year contracts and left the country after a few months; Guinean officials remarked bitterly that "the Americans could not take it here, our living conditions were not good enough for them." [2] If the Peace Corps, a U. S. Government agency, had sent these young teachers out, the venture would have been doomed even before it got on its feet, and the United States would have received a black eye in the opinion of the world. Private foreign aid agencies emphasize, therefore, that none but the cream of the crop should be chosen.

[1] *The New York Times,* January 23, 1961.
[2] *Ibid.,* February 3, 1961.

## CRITERIA FOR SELECTION

### Personal Characteristics

Senator Humphrey's "Youth Peace Corps" bill set an age range of from twenty-one and a half to thirty-two years, and the opinion of the private agencies interviewed, with few exceptions, is that twenty-one to thirty is the ideal span. Under twenty-one, it is felt, the prospective worker has not had enough experience to give him a sufficient background; by twenty-one, a young man or woman should have experienced enough of life to be able to adjust to new situations. After the thirty- to thirty-two-year range, effectiveness usually lessens, both physically and psychologically. Also, a person above that age has trouble adjusting to teamwork among new people, especially when his fellow workers are youths in their early twenties or of a completely different generation. However, the age problem will ultimately depend on the type of work to be done; the American Friends Service Committee and Operation Crossroads-Africa have found that boys and girls eighteen to twenty-one can be used satisfactorily in work-camp operations overseas. The Peace Corps *Fact Book*, on the other hand, states that volunteers will have a practical range of from eighteen to forty-five, with older people serving as instructors at training centers or as overseas supervisors. Actually, both Peace Corpsmen and private agency workers are of the opinion that the best age is twenty-five.

Should women go abroad as Peace Corps volunteers? Again, the early Humphrey bill omitted women from consideration, but the Peace Corps as now planned sees wide use for qualified persons regardless

47

of sex, and already several women have been chosen as Peace Corps trainees. The prototype International Voluntary Services have made it almost a hard and fast rule not to accept women, except where, in the case of married couples, both could qualify as a chief-of-party team. Most other agencies, however, say that there are many situations in which a woman can do a better job than a man can. In many Oriental countries where it is taboo for a woman to be treated by a male doctor or nurse, women have also been useful as instructors of home economics and other domestic arts. One of the basic problems overseas is diet. Occasionally, even where food is adequate, ignorance of food conservation and of how to prepare the simplest dishes results in a perpetual state of ill health for the Asian family.

A related problem is whether or not male and female volunteers should work in the same project. Many fear such a situation will result in failure because of the romantic temptations involved. However, both the Quakers and Operation Crossroads-Africa report that they have never had any great problem here. Stephen Carey says that, on the contrary, "Projects employing both men and women—especially if in a lonely outpost—are beneficial. Both morale and the tone of the work," he added, "are improved, without any unfortunate moral difficulties. The people we select have a firm religious background, and we have not had a single case of misbehavior. The only time when difficulties arose was when a boy and a girl on a project started going steady, and this partially disrupted the teamwork of the group. However, it only required adjustment by team members to the new situation, and happily this occurred." Mr. Carey continued by saying that the biggest problem of male and female vounteers is one of cross-cultural adjustment. Customs and dress in most countries are different from ours; girls in certain Latin-American and Oriental lands are not allowed to wear shorts or other abbreviated dress, and they must watch their step in their relationship with the local men. A situation that is considered innocent in the United States may, and often does, have very ugly connotations in Africa or Asia, for example.

Many married couples have expressed an interest in the Peace Corps. Can they be utilized? The official policy of the Peace Corps is that married couples may be used only when both partners are qualified, there are no marital difficulties, and they have no minor dependents. In line with this policy, a married couple from Massachusetts, both secondary schoolteachers, were among the twenty-nine trainees selected for the pilot project in Ghana. Several private agencies also require that married couples be married for a certain length of time. The reason is that they have had unfortunate experiences with couples who tended to use the work tour as a sort of prolonged honeymoon. One agency worker with years of experience added grimly that the "boondocks of Southeast Asia is not the best place for newlyweds to adjust to each other and to their new state of life."

With married couples the question arises as to what would happen if the wife were to become pregnant during the tour of duty. Professor Samuel P. Hayes of the University of Michigan has suggested that "assignments of those couples to whom this happens can be adapted to permit at least one of the couple to complete the full term of service, and perhaps to have

49

at least part-time service from the other member." [3] Peace Corps officials consider this solution impractical, however, and the general rule is that the couple would have to return to the United States. The only mitigating circumstances would be that the couple were financially well-off or that their place of duty were in a city where adequate facilities were available. But even there it is felt that a dangerous precedent would be set by exception to the firmly established rules that no outside income be allowed and that the work of the team take precedence over all other considerations.

## What Sort of Educational Background Is Desired?

The purpose of the Peace Corps is to provide "middle manpower" to underdeveloped nations that, on the one hand, receive the highly skilled technical assistance of ICA and the United Nations for such projects as hydroelectric dams and steel factories, while having, on the other hand, a large surplus of unskilled labor. What they lack is the "middle" or semi-skilled techniques of basic industry, agriculture and other occupations.

For these reasons, AFL-CIO officials feel that volunteers experienced in a particular skill, yet having no more than a high school education, might be used. Many people, either lacking an aptitude for formal studies or forced to leave school for various reasons, know their trades—in many instances, skills that cannot be learned in colleges—from A to Z, and are of the opinion that they could contribute badly needed techniques to the new nations.

However, there is a ground swell of doubt concern-

[3] *An International Peace Corps* (Washington, D.C.: Public Affairs Institute, 1961), p. 60.

ing the use of anyone except college graduates. There are even some who feel that anyone going overseas to instruct ought to have at least a master's degree. The first reason for this is a belief that a college education is usually a broadening experience that cannot be gotten elsewhere. Bread-and-butter issues are important to an Asian, but so, for that matter, are the intellectual and cultural sides of life; it is felt that a tradesman without a formal education will not be able to discuss such subjects on an adequate basis of equality with his counterparts.

In the second place, the Peace Corps, like the private agencies preceding it, will have to contend with the feelings of the host country. Many countries, it has been pointed out, may find it a bit insulting to be offered technicians with nothing more than high school diplomas. Countries such as India actually have a surplus of college-educated technicians in relation to their present needs or ability to absorb them. They might attack a non-college-trained assistance group on the grounds that it was competing with, not supplementing, local talent. Others feel that a non-college-educated volunteer is not the best to be had, as the Peace Corps advertises itself; the reasoning is, rightly or not, that if the person is so outstanding, why didn't he find some way to get his degree?

Many private agency officials feel that this is certainly true for the initial recruitment purposes of the Peace Corps, but that it would be too parochial a view in the long run, when the agency begins to expand its activities to meet the needs of the underdeveloped countries. The official Peace Corps policy is that *all qualified* volunteers will be used, regardless of formal education or the lack of it.

51

Tied in with educational qualifications is the volunteer's knowledge of foreign languages. The various International Voluntary Services and several other organizations do not require skill in the language of the host country, for the most part because such languages are "exotic" or little known. IVS has an intensive program of language study for the volunteer *after* he arrives at his post. Operation Crossroads-Africa, on the other hand, normally selects only those college students who are willing to add intensive language study to their normal work load *before* going to Africa. More important than an actual grasp of a particular language is skill in languages in general, or language aptitude. Service schools and certain universities have shown that a person with normal intelligence and some language aptitude can learn the basics of a particular language in as little as three to nine months of intensive training.

## General Experience Background

The Peace Corpsman will not be expected to be a jack-of-all-trades, but neither should he or she live in a world bounded only by a chosen specialty. Most college volunteers will have had only summer or part-time work experience, and in this case the examiner must consider extracurricular activities. In this category, for example, are work with a Boy Scout troop, counselor in a summer camp, tinkering with automobiles as a hobby, or organizing a political or charity drive. When a companion of the late Mahatma Gandhi of India heard of the Peace Corps, she advised the United States to send youths who know how to laugh and make other people laugh. Asia, she said, knows enough of sadness so that there is no need for serious-faced boys and girls to teach more of it to her people. For this reason, although Peace Corps work will not be play, it is considered essential that volunteers know how to participate in games and how to dance, if only a few basic steps. Entertainment in very many other ways will be out of the question—there are no electrical outlets in the bush of Africa or the jungles of Southeast Asia for a stereo hi-fi set; as housing space is at a premium, books and magazines will be few. This is far afield from technical competence, but it is nonetheless important.

It is hoped that volunteers who have worked with private agencies or colleges in Peace Corps type operations will give their services to the new agency. Others considered valuable by the Peace Corps are people who have lived for a considerable time overseas, either as business representatives or armed service dependents. Anyone who has had to adjust to a foreign culture will already have overcome the initial barrier, although different cultures raise different problems. Not so valuable are tourist trips of the ordinary sort; no tourist gains much more than a superficial insight into a foreign culture.

## Personality

What are the personal qualities needed for success in overseas operations such as the Peace Corps? Harlan Cleveland decided that the five most relevant elements are: technical skill, belief in mission, cultural empathy, a sense for politics, and organizational ability.[4] The National Council of the Churches of Christ lists integrity of character, a high sense of values,

---

[4] *The Overseas Americans* by H. Cleveland (New York: McGraw-Hill, 1960), p. 263.

motivation for service, and willingness to do a hard job. The Quakers have similar standards: maturity, adaptability, religious motivation, ability to get along with others, ability to evaluate the total situation or perspective, and a sense of humor. However defined, they all add up to the secret ingredients that make for success. A volunteer is not expected to have all of them in the fullest degree, but he is expected to show that he possesses more of these qualities than would be needed to succeed at home.

## Motivation and Ideals

All Peace Corpsmen will be expected to have a higher motive for service than the almighty dollar or love of adventure. What the private agencies have looked for in a recruit is a humanitarian zeal to help his fellow man, combined with a willingness to do a hard job. The pie-in-the-sky idealists are usually disillusioned soon after they arrive at their posts. Fighting mosquitoes in the middle of the night and working in swamp water up to your knees in mud is hardly a very glamorous aspect. Working with a peasant who is wondering where his next meal is coming from or trying to replace ancient attitudes of fatalism leaves no room for the anti-Communist crusader or the religious fanatic. But the cynic will be out of place, too. One has to have a pioneering spirit of some sort to maintain the spirit of enthusiasm needed in the face of frustration after frustration. Many volunteers make the mistake of thinking that they will see immediate success in their particular project; on the contrary, it is all too seldom that the fruits of labor are only realized in an overseas project long after the technician has gone home.

A common motive for engaging in such work is an interest in broadening one's education and experience. The worker in Tanganyika should try to learn from the Tanganyikan culture, instead of going over just to teach others his own country's methods. A one-way exchange is no exchange at all, and this is part of the reason for the well-publicized failure of so many efforts to teach new techniques to ancient cultures. This tendency, as a whole, is called cultural empathy, for it is a sympathy with other cultures. The foreigner working in another land has to learn not to measure everything by his own or his country's standards, and he must also resist the ever-present temptation to compare the ideals of his own culture with the often harsh realities of another.

## Maturity

Maturity, of course, combines all these considerations, but by maturity in specific is meant a considered and good judgment, thoughtfulness and consideration of others, a spirit of co-operation in working as a member of a team, and, one might add, tact, humility and patience. Many of these are qualities Americans are not noted for particularly, but they are qualities that must be had and be practiced. An insecure, argumentative and opinionated individual, well known for a back-slapping camaraderie, is the worst possible volunteer, although in many parts of the world he happens to be the American stereotype.

## Tolerance

Tolerance is a part of getting along with others, and it cannot be overemphasized. If a volunteer goes overseas with prejudices on any grounds—racial, political, religious, national or class—he jeopardizes the entire operation, especially of a foreign-aid enterprise such as the Peace Corps. Many of the newer nations have deep dislikes and misconceptions of America. A few unfavorable reports of events in Little Rock, Arkansas, or Montgomery, Alabama, often are more persuasive than forty years of painstaking agency work. The Corpsman will have to fight his own natural inclinations and swallow his anger when he runs up against resentment and insult from those he has come to work with and assist.

## Ingenuity

Very important is ingenuity. It is this aptitude that finds solutions to the vexing problems confronting the Corpsman. Something of the spirit in the belief that the impossible takes only a little longer to achieve than the difficult should belong to the overseas worker. Though he is an English language teacher in the bush of Africa, he must also know how to help repair a plow or perhaps use crude materials to fix a well. This is one of the reasons why the International Voluntary Services insist on recruits with rural backgrounds.

## Loyalty and Security

The touchy question of Communist infiltration has been brought up persistently by critics and supporters alike. In the spring of 1961, the National Conference on Youth Service Abroad came out against either a security clearance or a loyalty oath for volunteers. The reason, they argued, is that Peace Corpsmen will not be political agents and therefore should make no affirmation of loyalty other than the standard passport requirements for Americans traveling abroad. Quaker officials fear that security checks will arouse the suspicions of neutralist nations that volunteers are actually undercover CIA agents.

Peace Corps Director Shriver gave the official view of this problem in two separate radio-television panel sessions. In the first,[5] his questioner was Republican Senator Hugh Scott of Pennsylvania:

SENATOR SCOTT: Will you have an FBI check [of the Corps applicant]?

MR. SHRIVER: We're working very closely with Mr. [J. Edgar] Hoover. . . . We're also working with the Civil Service Commission, and I can assure you and any of your correspondents . . . that every effort will be made to protect the Peace Corps against any infiltration by foreign groups of any kind.

SENATOR SCOTT: Does that mean that there will be an FBI clearance on all of these people?

MR. SHRIVER: That will be determined by the Director of the FBI, not by me.

SENATOR SCOTT: If not by the FBI, will there be some form of security clearance?

MR. SHRIVER: Definitely.

Later, a student on *Youth Wants to Know* [6] said that in view of the sophistication and thorough indoctrination of Communist agents, wasn't it possible that American youths might be influenced by them? Mr. Shriver answered with an emphatic no, and said:

[5] *Your Senators Report*, broadcast jointly with Senator Joseph S. Clark over Pennsylvania radio and television stations, April 2, 1961.

[6] WABC-TV, New York City, July 9, 1961.

You have to remember we're sending over people who are mature and well-balanced and well-trained, and they're under leadership that's going to be very able, so that when they're in a country, we will be seeing what they're doing . . . they know a lot about the United States. I'm not scared that they're going to be turned into Communists simply because they see a Communist. Perhaps they'll turn the Communist into Americans.

A few of the voluntary agencies have had close calls with Communist-oriented individuals. None, however, have slipped through their tightly controlled selection processes or, in the case of those having contracts with ICA, through the government security investigations.

## Selection of Leaders

Dr. J. S. Noffsinger of IVS called this the "great bottleneck." All of the private agencies insist that a team can be made up of outstanding rank-and-file volunteers, yet fall apart because it lacks proper leadership. On the other hand, an outstanding leader can take a bunch of raw, even mediocre, recruits and weld them into an effective work unit.

If the rank-and-file are the cream of the crop, then the group leader has to be extraordinarily qualified. It is rare that a team of leaderless followers will close ranks effectively when the chips are down. The quality of the leader will largely determine the group's success and, in the final analysis, decide the fate of the venture.

In 1960, Dr. Harold Isaacs of M.I.T.'s Center for International Studies surveyed the personnel problem on the spot for Operation Crossroads-Africa. In stark, realistic terms, his confidential report pinpointed many of the pitfalls that confront the Crossroaders— and the Peace Corps. He noted that there is no infallible litmus test for selecting the right leaders, but he said, "The evidence does suggest, however, that the better leader is more likely a man than a woman, a younger man rather than an older man, near enough in age [to the group] to pitch in with the work and enjoy the more active parts of the fun, yet old enough to be plainly senior to the young adults in his charge. . . . Who knows and likes young people . . . who knows how to be careful without being overcautious, how to deal sensitively with individual needs and problems while respecting the needs of the group."

The petty tyrant, the study advised, is anathema. Group participants rated leaders "excellent" or "good" on the basis of how they combined democratic use of their authority with skill and common sense in dealing with unexpected and difficult situations. "The leader," Dr. Isaacs summed up, "should have the ultimate power of veto and decision, but he should operate in a way that requires him never to invoke it."

Just as important as his relation to the group is the leader's verve and sensitivity in getting to know the people of the host country and the tangibles and intangibles of any local situation. Many problems arise out of the difference between what people *say* and what they actually *do*. Americans, for example, are noted for their punctuality, so that around the world there are now *two* concepts of time instead of just one: American time and local time. If the leader doesn't understand what a problem is all about, then

59

those in his command will almost certainly also fail. An overseas technician with more than forty-five years of field experience observed that village people are nobody's fools; they're keen judges of character and quickly separate the real from the phony. With a centuries-ingrained shrewdness, they have no qualms about exploiting a leaderless situation, especially where the leader—supposedly the spokesman of the group—cannot give his workers an effective example of how to deal with their host counterparts.

In this connection, almost to a man, the private agencies insist that leaders should be chosen from persons having overseas experience, preferably in a leadership capacity of one kind or another. Naturally, the supply of such personnel is limited, and it is expected that at least some of the leaders will have to come from Peace Corpsmen who excel in the orientation and training period.

If Peace Corps standards are as rigid as those of the private voluntary groups, its leaders will be top notch.

In light of the exhaustive nature of the selection process, skeptics are dubious that, for the modest financial rewards involved, many youths will want to apply. A further complication, it is thought, is the threat of the military draft upon completion of Peace Corps service. One Peace Corps official has said frankly that this unresolved question "will make my selection problem much simpler. Those who still have the motivation, the gumption, the adventuresomeness and the flexibility will select themselves. They will see two or three years overseas helping others help themselves as an opportunity not to be missed, as an addition to their own qualifications, not just as an interlude or waste of time. I will still have thousands more applications than I can handle."

# CHAPTER 2

# WHAT SORT OF PREPARATION?

The Peace Corps will involve placing large numbers of Americans in day-to-day, person-to-person contact with the peoples of the underdeveloped nations. Too often in the past, however, many technicians have found themselves suddenly uprooted from the familiar surroundings of their native America and thrust into the midst of a foreign locale, ignorant of its culture and special problems. The reason is obvious: little or no advance training. This is true not only of American private enterprise operations overseas, but also of government programs. It was not until the Foreign Service Act of 1946 that any systematic training was provided the professional U. S. Foreign Service officer! It took two world wars and innumerable international conferences to get Congress—and public opinion—to recognize American involvement in the world arena as more than a temporary aberration.

The dangers of inadequate preparation for overseas work have tragic and comic aspects alike. Lee St. Lawrence, advance scout for the first Peace Corps project, learned that lesson 250 miles back in the remote bush of Tanganyika. Tribesmen told him of a geologist who had been killed merely for breaking up some rocks. His crime was that he had failed to get permission first from the local chief.[1] On the more comic side, a Catholic priest tells this one on himself. Some years ago, newly assigned as a missionary, he joined villagers in hacking away at the jungle. He later noticed that, despite the blistering hot day, one young girl was putting in more than her share of the work, and he decided the only suitable recognition of such industry would be to invite her to dinner. That done, he was surprised no end when the girl's father grimly informed him that a wedding was in the offing for the two. It seems that, in that part of Africa, to invite a single girl to dinner is the same as a proposal to marriage. The priest wryly noted that it took some real talking to extricate himself from that situation!

## Orientation

Strictly speaking, orientation and training are two separate phases of the preparation for overseas work. Orientation is concerned primarily with studies of the culture of the host country, the history and special conditions in the surrounding area as a whole (i.e., Latin America, the Near East, Africa, Asia), United States history and public policy, and human relations. The goal of training, on the other hand, is to provide or improve the various professional skills, such as teaching methods and special job techniques, that the volunteer will need in his work, and to drill him intensively in the language of the country that he will serve and in general linguistic studies.

[1] New York *Herald Tribune,* April 30, 1961.

63

Since most young Americans going to a so-called "exotic" land like Ghana or India will have either very little idea of what to expect or a lot of stereotyped misconceptions, it is obvious that the orientation period will be the more important of the two. A newcomer is expected to commit the usual number of mistakes during his first two or three months on the scene, but it is hoped that a good stiff orientation will both lessen their harmful impact and familiarize the trainee enough to acquire before too long a time the *expertise* of an "old hand." However, as one IVS technician wrote recently, "Theory is of little value in working with peasant-type people. No amount of stateside training will be of as much benefit," he said, "as on-the-job training, because to learn the feel of the country and how the people think, you must actually be there—not sitting in a classroom 3,000 miles away."

The majority of experts consulted for this study disagree with this judgment although they grant it a certain validity. One of the primary reasons is that here in the United States there are numerous facilities adequate for intensive Peace Corps training, whereas they are practically nonexistent in would-be host countries. According to the American Council on Education's survey of 468 colleges and universities, 43.5 per cent have special international programs available, while 61.7 per cent are prepared to accept Peace Corps contracts for training volunteers. Another reason why it would not be practical to omit orientation and training in the United States is the outcry it would arouse from both supporters and critics of the Peace Corps. It would merely confirm skeptics in their impression that the new agency is just another costly boondoggle which will cost us the respect of the world by sending over droves of naïve, untrained youths.

A recommended course of orientation includes six main areas of study:

1. The history, culture and institutions of the host country within the framework of the surrounding region.
2. Current events and modern problems in the life of the country.
3. The differences between cultures.
4. General human relations and group psychology.
5. Practical living conditions.
6. United States history, culture and institutions, plus American public policy and the mission of the Peace Corps.

## The Host Country

Since people's reactions are determined largely by previous conditioning, a worker overseas must be aware that his activities are being thought of—judged, really—according to the standards of the country and the village where he is living. These are more often than not quite different from the standards to which Americans are accustomed. To know just what the local citizenry's impression is and what relationships with them really are, it is necessary to understand their viewpoint. The foreigner does not have to adopt that viewpoint, but his effectiveness depends on his being aware of it and sensitive to it. He cannot accomplish this unless he has studied the history which has conditioned the culture and the institutions of the people with whom he works. Neither can he understand their problems and the day-to-day events in their nation's life unless he first tries to place them within their own cultural context—not through the eyes of American culture, but instead by putting himself in their shoes and then asking himself how they would see it.

Much of the traditional pageantry and social customs in underdeveloped countries is colorful and fascinating to the foreign eye, but there are many others which are not. If the Peace Corpsman who goes to work in a country is largely ignorant of its less-attractive customs and the reasons behind them, he will soon leave in disgust and frustration. Dr. Noffsinger of IVS expressed particular concern about this problem. The impatient foreign technician, seeing the disease and poverty rampant in a country such as Egypt, for example, decides to solve these ancient curses of mankind with one fell swoop. "Aha," he says in effect to the Arab fellah, "I see people are dying like flies in this province from malaria. I'll get some DDT spray and kill the mosquitoes that spread it." The peasant just shrugs his shoulders and protests that nothing can be done about it, it is the will of Allah. The foreigner brushes his protest aside as superstition, takes his spray gun and eradicates the deadly malaria from the village. The people are healthy now, but, as Dr. Noffsinger pointed out, two problems have sprung up where once there was one. The peasant has lost both the moorings which were his faith and his confidence in himself, and his culture now has no meaning to him. Instead of feeling grateful to the foreign technician, he now resents him. The fast-moving world of modern technology has swept the underdeveloped peoples into a bewildering whirlwind of change and into an awakening to the Darwin concept of "survival of the fittest." Some anthropologists feel that the angry nationalisms erupting in those nations are partly in reaction to the increasing displacement of the old values without replacing them with something equally strong.

Customs like this are not easy to change, and patience combined with understanding is the only answer. Prime Minister Jawaharlal Nehru of India has long butted his head against the granitelike problems of the caste system and overpopulation, and, it might seem, with little sign of accomplishment. His social workers have discovered after thirteen years in the field that these things cannot be changed overnight. And workers with the private voluntary agencies have often felt equally frustrated in trying to get vital projects off the ground, only to find themselves stymied by a notion universal among the less developed peoples—the disdain of the educated elite for common labor and contact with the soil.

Forewarned is forearmed. By learning the obstacles ahead, the Peace Corpsman will realize all the sooner that it is only possible to attack them by approaching his work in an alien culture with the greatest degree of caution and tact.

## Practical Living Conditions

Aside from cultural differences, there are equally practical, perhaps more down-to-earth, considerations. What kind of diet will the volunteer find in the area? How and where will he live? What community life can he look forward to? How sanitary are the people, and how is he expected to adapt to their

67

habits? What medical care will be provided in case of illness or injury?

Most of these questions are answered adequately by the case histories in Part III of this book, but an orientation program will have to answer them in detail, with a slant toward the locality where the volunteer will serve. An agricultural technician with the International Voluntary Services in Vietnam was asked recently what living conditions a Peace Corpsman might expect there. He wrote:

> It has been the mistake of some to believe that you would live exactly as the local people do. If this were the case, most Youth Corps members would suffer from countless diseases. We most certainly do not have the same resistance as the people of the country. It would be foolish not to boil water and take other sanitary measures.
>
> In my visits to tribal villages I eat rats, snakes or whatever they put before me; I drink rice wine and I sleep in a grass shack or in the middle of the jungle. I can assure you that it takes a certain amount of adjustment and that such an everyday pattern would be quite a strain. You can, however, live on the local level with some variation and improvement over the way the tribesmen do things, and by doing so, you can show them how to improve their way of life.

Despite such "concessions" as boiling water and putting up screens to ward off mosquitoes, Peace Corps Director Sargent Shriver was not overstating his point when he said that life in the armed forces may be more glamorous and much safer. Upon returning from an inspection of conditions in the West African Republic of Senegal, Reverend Bill Moyers advised Shriver in a memorandum to include a public sanitation expert and a health official with each Peace Corps team working there.

## American Studies

In an earlier chapter, reference was made to criticism by Jack Gould, *The New York Times* television critic, that several overseas volunteers were practically ignorant of world affairs. Prior to the 1960 World Youth Festival, a non-Communist organization found itself confronted with a similar problem: the youths applying as American delegates to the Communist-sponsored affair had little or no background in United States history and current events. Past experiences at the 1957 Festival in Moscow resulted in a virtual rout for the unsophisticated few Americans who represented democratic opinion. Unprepared for serious debate and offset by numerous Communist-led delegates from the West, they were, for the most part, unable to give a persuasive defense of American institutions and policies. The clinching irony is that this was just a short time after the Russian suppression of Hungary's revolt, when the shoe should have been on the other foot.

It is inevitable that Peace Corpsmen will run up against barbed criticisms of America by hostile neutralists and professional agitators. There will also be honest, though no less loaded, questions by sincere and friendly hosts. Race riots in the Southern United States, the ill-fated Cuban invasion and the scandal of depressed West Virginia in our affluent country—these are only a few of the subjects American representatives encounter abroad. The Peace Corps has warned prospective recruits to expect a reception of this sort, but in an information bulletin released last April it cautioned that although "trainees will be expected to acquire background on political, economic, social, and religious institutions abroad (as well as those in the United States), they may not exhibit partisanship with respect to issues and organizations in these fields abroad." [2] Harlan Cleveland, the present Assistant Secretary of State for International Affairs and former dean of Syracuse University, has seemingly taken issue with the official Peace Corps stand. Referring to the give and take of democratic debate within American society, he contends that representatives abroad should express their own mature views and, by doing so, "glory in our own pluralism." Sargent Shriver has scoffed at the fear that Corpsmen will parrot a predetermined government line, and he said that volunteers "no doubt will have to withstand Communist attacks . . . but we are not going over there to preach for a religion or a political system; we are going over there to work." [3] The Peace Corps plans a comprehensive series of refresher courses in American history, culture and arts, as well as current events, economic and political development, and international affairs. With that sort of background, volunteers should hardly be at a loss for words in any debate.

## Training

Of the first 4,800 applicants for the Peace Corps, a wide variety of professional and technical skills turned up. A partial rundown reads as follows:

[2] *Educational Institutions and the Peace Corps,* April 1, 1961.
[3] The Baltimore *Sun,* May 18, 1961.

| SKILLS | NUMBER [4] |
|---|---|
| Surveyors | 205 |
| Bulldozers | 172 |
| Farm equipment | 580 |
| Tractors | 712 |
| Automobile mechanics | 406 |
| Electricians | 295 |
| Plumbers | 259 |
| Carpenters | 616 |
| Masons | 193 |
| Metal workers | 196 |
| Biologists | 370 |
| Chemists | 473 |
| Registered nurses | 270 |

Language skills were also quite high. To qualify for fluency in a foreign language, a student should be able to do at least two of the following: Give a short talk, read a newspaper, write a letter, understand a discussion. The requirements were met by more than two thousand students of four major European languages—Spanish, French, Italian and Portuguese—and fifty-eight qualified in Hindu, Urdu, Chinese and Arabic.

Obviously, most if not all of these skills will have to be adapted to the particular locale, as conditions often vary greatly from country to country and even within the country itself. The job to be done may require even further adaptation. For this, intensive classroom and work-experience training must be provided.

In addition, many volunteers have only a rudi-

[4] These figures include only those highly skilled and experienced in their work.

71

mentary or merely theoretical knowledge of their specialties. An adequate training program will have to tone up and develop the particular skill. The graduate from a liberal arts college who wants to teach English in a foreign country will undergo special courses in the English language and in teaching methods. If he speaks a language, he will have to study the local dialect if he is to make any sense at all to his pupils.

The problem does not end there, however, and this is where *the* necessary ingredient comes into play. Call it ingenuity or problem solving, it all amounts to the same thing: common horse sense. A good illustration is this excerpt from the diary of a voluntary agency worker:

When I first arrived in ——, I thought of myself as a teacher of English. But I soon learned other tasks were ahead for me.

My school consisted of a small one-room hut. My heart sank when I looked in to find not a single desk or chair. The village elder, as if by way of explanation, told me that the building previously had been used as a storehouse for crops. Night was approaching, so I decided to just get a good night's sleep and worry about it tomorrow.

The next morning, I assembled a squad of local men, and we went to work. With a few rusty tools and lots of elbow grease, we converted a few old citrus crates into halfway decent benches and a small lectern. A week later I was able to get hold of a sheet of tin and a bucket of black paint to improvise a blackboard. What tin and paint was left over I made into five small slates to give out as prizes for my harder-working pupils.

Since everyone was required to work in the fields

in the afternoon, I could hold classes only a half day at a time. I soon found myself planting, plowing and carrying water from the nearby creek, when I wasn't grading papers and preparing my next day's lesson.

The tiny hut soon became too small for my students, who shyly trickled in, by twos and threes, from neighboring villages. I tried to hold classes out of doors, but the insects and the intermittent rain and hot sun discouraged that fast. The next time I visited the capital, I asked the USOM [5] if they could get an Ellston block-making machine for me. With that, a few bags of cement, some lime and the sand in the village, I soon had enough blocks to construct a $40 \times 40$ foot schoolhouse. I didn't know what accomplishment really meant until I walked in for classes the morning after and found the entire village assembled there to express their thanks.

Of course, not every Peace Corpsman is so mechanically inclined as to be a jack-of-all-trades in addition to his normal work. This is where a good training program steps in. Working with a common-sense individual, they can train him in job techniques by using simulated work situations in the classroom and in the field. That is why training sites such as our Indian reservations, the depressed areas and rugged camping trips have been suggested as part of the Stateside preparation for Peace Corps work. A volunteer should be taught the basic elements of gardening, home economics and personal hygiene, even if his main work isn't in that field. Why? In the first place, he may need them in his own day-to-day life, and secondly so that

[5] United States Operations Mission.

he can pass on some of this practical learning to his native counterpart or his pupils, as the case may be.

## What about Language Studies?

Ever since the Russians fired Sputnik, the first space rocket, Americans have been concerned about their proficiency in foreign languages. Russian, which at the end of World War II was not widely taught, has now soared to one of the principal choices for study in universities and adult education programs. And some precocious tots in the primary grades are lisping *"nyet"* long before they have mastered Mother Goose rhymes.

Just how important *is* a foreign language? The overseasman, Harlan Cleveland believes, should study at least one language even if he can't master it.[6] The differences between cultures are so great that ignorance of a language often is a barrier to international understanding. The late President Franklin D. Roosevelt bemoaned this fact in speaking of his wartime relations with Russian dictator Joseph Stalin. "Unfortunately," he said, "the Marshal and I have no common language, and a shade of meaning or an intonation is often lost, even through the best of interpreters." [7]

Sometimes, however, the language problem is overstated and gets woefully out of perspective. Mr. Cleveland came to this conclusion when he protested that language "ought to be viewed as an important subhead under cultural empathy, and our linguistic renaissance should not preclude our giving adequate

[6] *The Overseas Americans* by H. Cleveland (New York: McGraw-Hill, 1960), p. 263.

[7] Henry Field, "How F.D.R. Did His Homework," *Saturday Review,* July 8, 1961.

educational attention to other elements of effective overseas performance." [8] No man should be sent to a hardship post like Senegal if he has a Ph.D. in French but none of the practical skills or the temperament needed.

Language training for Peace Corps work should be geared to the particular country or locality, but it should also be flexible enough to meet changing needs. Most experts are of the opinion that it should last from six weeks to six months, depending on the language itself and the individual's prior experience. The Army language school at The Presidium in Monterey, California, considers six months the necessary time to give an American an adequate command of a European language, but almost a year is required for Oriental languages. However, the needs of the Peace Corps are different from those of specialists in the armed forces, and this was recently explained by Sargent Shriver, the Director of the Peace Corps, on a New York television panel: [9]

QUESTION: Mr. Shriver, isn't it virtually impossible to learn a completely foreign tongue sufficiently in the normal training course of about six to eight weeks? And don't you feel that the whole training program is rushed a little too much for 100 per cent effectiveness?

MR. SHRIVER: Well, in the first place, we're not trying to teach a whole foreign language in six to eight weeks. I agree with you, that's impossible. What we're attempting to do in two or three months in this country is to give the foundation so that you can learn the language successfully when you go

[8] *The Overseas Americans,* Ibid.
[9] *Youth Wants To Know,* WABC-TV, July 9, 1961.

abroad. Also, I would like you to know that in the foreign country—in each foreign country— there will be a training program in that country. For example, in Tanganyika, there's going to be a two-month training program for our people after they arrive, and during that time the training in the language—Swahili—will continue. So that, before our volunteers are actually at work in Tanganyika, they will have had three or four months of intensive training in the foreign language. We think this will be enough to make it useful for them and worth the effort that we put into it. . . .

Learning the language of your host has two values. First, its result will be the broadening of one's own experience and horizons, and secondly it expresses a certain respect for your foreign work-associate and his culture. Neutralist intellectuals who have toured the Soviet Union make much of the fact that the Russians have a special institution devoted solely to the cultures and languages of Africa. The United States cannot do less.

A training program is only as good as the people who staff it and the selection process which has preceded it. If both meet the rigid standards necessary for an overseas venture like the Peace Corps, then it can be considered adequate. In fact, leaders of the voluntary services are quick to stress that the training program should be regarded as part of the whole selection process, a trial period to precede actual acceptance into the Peace Corps. Sargent Shriver accepted their advice and has compared the new agency to a baseball team, with the manager always ready and able to yank out a player before he ruins the game. The fewer the misfits, the better the chances for the Peace Corps to succeed in its mission.

# CHAPTER 3

# PEACE CORPS
## TRAINING IN ACTION

Tanganyika, the first country selected for Peace Corps work, is a British-administered trust territory in East Africa. The average American knows of Tanganyika only as the site of Henry Stanley's Lake Victoria and the fabled Mount Kilimanjaro. This December, however, the country becomes the 22nd African nation to gain independence since World War II, and will assume a pivotal role in emerging Africa's political life.

Both the Peace Corps and Tanganyika's Prime Minister Julius Nyerere regard the project as a serious part of the country's development; the current three-year plan was specially redrafted to include Peace Corps assistance.

The economy of Tanganyika is primarily agricultural, yet only 9 per cent of her land is under cultivation. The job of the Peace Corps volunteers will be twofold. The four civil engineers and twenty surveyors will build small "feeder" roads to connect outlying farms with the marketplace, and they will participate in such major projects as the Mwanza/Musoma road, now being constructed through Development Loan Fund assistance. Six geologists are to study the land and rock formations to provide detailed maps for future exploitation of the as yet untapped mineral resources. When field work is not feasible, the road builders will teach Tanganyikan apprentices, and the geologists will work in regional offices of the geological survey division of the Tanganyika government.

To prepare the vounteers for their two years in Tanganyika, the Peace Corps has set up a rigid 4½-month training program involving three separate phases.

# I

## TEXAS WESTERN COLLEGE, EL PASO, TEXAS
### (Eight Weeks)

One of the primary reasons why Texas Western was chosen is that the terrain of southwest Texas is very much like Tanganyika. This is important because a full week has been given over to surpervised field trips in which the prospective recruits put their skills to work.

The over-all director of the El Paso program is Dr. Clyde Kelsey, a Texas Western psychology professor, and the Peace Corps is represented by Robert W. Iversen of Pennsylvania State College, an instructor in American studies and international affairs.

The staff assembled is an impressive one. The Tanganyikan area specialists are Professor James B. Christensen of Michigan's Wayne State University and Dr. Margaret Bates of Goddard College in Vermont. Professor Christensen is an anthropologist with ex-

**79**

tensive experience in West Africa and speaks fluent Swahili, Tanganyika's principal language. When he joined the El Paso training team, he brought along as training aids over 2,000 slides and movies that he shot in northern Tanganyika in recent years. Dr. Bates, meanwhile, is an Oxford Ph. D. and an expert on Tanganyikan politics; Oxford University plans to publish her recent study, *Tanganyika under British Administration*, sometime next year.

The surveyors and civil engineers among the volunteers are under the supervision of Texas Western and University of Texas staff experts, while Scotsborn Daniel Harkin, a geologist seasoned by many years' work in Tanganyika, is geological instructor.

The training is divided roughly into 40 per cent technical, 25 per cent area studies, 15 per cent medical training and physical conditioning, 10 per cent American institutions and international affairs, and 10 per cent language training. Technical training is further divided into classroom, laboratory work, and the work-practice field trips. Area orientation, or Tanganyikan studies, includes lectures and discussion periods, films and assigned readings on the history, culture, politics and economic development plans of Tanganyika. Medical training involves first-aid and disease instruction, while about 70 hours of calisthenics and other exercises compose the physical conditioning. The language program is intensive, but its main purpose is to make the volunteer familiar with, not fluent in, Swahili to prepare him for the main course to come in Tanganyika.

That the training is no Sunday pleasure outing is emphasized to the would-be Corpsman at once. First, he is greeted with a stiff physical examination, psychological testing, and a long series of vaccinations against local diseases. Every morning thereafter he is awakened at 5:30 to start a day that may not end until he has finished cramming at midnight for the next day's session. On Sunday—if he is sufficiently dedicated—he will spend his day off in further studying, reading another book or listening to tapes in Swahili. And much of his "spare" time is spent in discussing the program and the prospects ahead with his fellow recruits.

## II

### FIELD TRAINING CENTER, PUERTO RICO
### *(26 Days)*

Those who survive the El Paso training will proceed, after a brief respite, to Puerto Rico. There the Peace Corps has set up a camp twelve miles inland from the port of Arecibo. The site is 1,000 feet above sea level in a mountain range and a dense rain forest.

For Peace Corps officials, Arecibo has four basic advantages:

1. *Climate*—a taste of what to expect.
2. *Community development program*—Puerto Rico, under Commonwealth Governor Luis Munoz Marin, has established rural improvement work in around 350 villages.
3. *"Spartan living"*—staff and volunteers sleep in tents, and only the minimum necessary equipment will be available.
4. *Foreign language and culture situation*—living and working among a people who speak a dif-

81

ferent language and have different customs and foods.

Like El Paso, round-the-clock will be the order of the day. Peace Corps officials emphasize, however, that theirs is not a military-type "boot camp" training. What they hope to develop in the volunteers is an "inner discipline" and sheer physical and mental endurance. "The job," one instructor said, "is how to make these fellows realize they've got more in them than they ever dreamt. Of course, we have to work on the assumption that these guys already have something to start off with."

And a tough program it is. Physical conditioning will play a major part in toughening the trainees, and this is the task of Forrest Evashevsky, the athletic director for the University of Iowa who volunteered as a consultant with the Peace Corps. Under the general category of swimming come life-saving and survival techniques, as well as guiding a kayak through the swift-moving waters of local streams. Then there are the "rock-climbing" and aerial obstacle courses, which involve scaling nearby cliffs and climbing ropes across rivers and chasms. Soon after the volunteer arrives, he is treated to classroom studies of map and compass direction-finding, and that same evening he is taken into the jungle to make his own way back by a specified time the next morning.

Since the Tanganyika group will train in Puerto Rico during the hurricane season, their medical and survival training may come in handy. They will be given first-aid situations, during which they will discover simulated "wounded and dying" along jungle paths. Experts will judge their reaction and approach to the problem at hand. If the hurricane *does* hit the area, they will have to worry not only about their own survival, but also the rescue of the local villagers. Shelters will have to be constructed, food provided, and first-aid and transport to nearby hospitals will have to be given those caught by the storm. Woven throughout the entire experience is the idea of service to others, rather than self-preservation.

In addition to a continuous, though less intensive, course in Swahili, the volunteer will have evening lectures, which will cover three areas:

1. *"Critical incident."*
2. *Current events*—includes discussion of the civil rights problem in the United States, the Cuban invasion, the U-2 incident and other U. S. policy questions, as well as the Hungarian Revolution, the Pasternak affair, etc. The object, Peace Corps officials say, is not to "brainwash" those we send to work overseas but to make them aware of the several sides to each question, in case they get involved in similar discussions.
3. *Human relations*—differences in individual and group relationships in a foreign country.

Of the three, the "critical incident" is perhaps the most important. How is the Peace Corpsman to react in a delicate situation? For example, the Corpsman and his native work-associate, or counterpart, are sitting down and talking over a local brew. In comes an American contractor, frustrated by problems and tired by long days without sleep. He begins ranting and raving about everything in general and against Tanganyika in particular, and the Corpsman tries without success to quiet him down or send him away.

Instead, he only gets worse. Does the Corpsman, as one consultant commented, crawl under the nearest table and try to pretend the embarrassing situation doesn't exist? Or does he grab the contractor by the collar and drag him away? These are the type of questions the Corpsman will have to solve himself.

The training in Puerto Rico will not just involve theory or experiment, however. They will spend about 4½ days participating in community development projects, not in large groups but in pairs. Each pair will be put aboard a *publico* (Puerto Rican bus) and go to an assigned village. There they will live with a Puerto Rican family and work in co-operation with and under the direction of the local community development chief. Whether they build pigsties or plan forest trails will be up to him.

Next in technical training is site improvement. Here experts take the trainees out into the forest, and they are graded on their choice of sites, culverts, assessing forest acreage, and other tests. This phase is a practical carry-over of the week-long El Paso field trip.

The final test of endurance consists of two hiking expeditions, the first for 1½ days and the second for 3 days. The volunteers travel by foot for considerable distances along roads, trails and through forest maze. The reason for the Herculean nature of the effort is to force the volunteer to pit his wit and what he has learned so far against the unknown in order to survive.

The only casualties expected from such rigorous training are a case or two of dysentery, some sprains and bruises, perhaps a broken bone—and some of the trainees who will not be able to make the grade. Its object, however, is to assure that the Peace Corpsman will not only have been trained technically, but also that he will learn the real meaning and purpose of the Peace Corps.

## III

### NATURAL RESOURCES SCHOOL, TENGERU, TANGANYIKA
*(Seven Weeks)*

The Government of Tanganyika has set up a training program of its own at this technical school located at the foot of Mount Kilimanjaro. Graduates of both El Paso and Arecibo will study Swahili four hours a day, listen to further orientation lectures on Tanganyika, and take part in supervised field work in their specialty. Most of the instructors will be Tanganyikan.

With that final phase of training behind them, Project Tanganyika will begin work on assignment by the end of November.

# PART THREE

---

# WORK IN THE FIELD:

# CASE HISTORIES

# OF PROJECTS

# CHAPTER 1

## IVS/INDOCHINA

The Program that Peace Corps officials credit with a virtual blueprint of future operations is the International Voluntary Services, which began in 1953 as the godchild of the late Secretary of State, John Foster Dulles. IVS works under contract with ICA and several private foundations, and right now has technicians in Cambodia, Laos, Liberia and Vietnam; formerly, it also operated in Egypt, Ghana, Iraq, Jordan and Nepal. Its entire staff consists of four full-time and two part-time workers at the office run by Dr. J. S. Noffsinger in Washington, D.C.

To give an idea of what IVS men have been up against and of how they have gone about their tasks, this chapter is in the form of "newsletters" filed by a fictional IVS technician. The place is Lonkam, a mythical country somewhere in Southeast Asia, and the characters are all fictional. Though IVS/Indochina is a composite of several localities and projects, all incidents mentioned in the letters actually occurred —all were taken from actual field reports and newsletters on file with IVS, and nothing has been exaggerated. The fictional form of the chapter was taken at the request of Dr. Noffsinger to avoid identification with particular projects or persons.

*Ba-Vienh, Lonkam*
*September 6, 1959*

DEAR FOLKS,

Hello from Ba-Vienh! Here's my first newsletter. I'd like to reply to each of you separately, but since that's out of the question IVS mimeographs copies for my friends.

Six weeks ago I was happily surprised to get a telegram from IVS headquarters in Washington saying "Join team at once in Kansas City. . . ." I had been dickering for several months with IVS to get the two-year assignment as an agricultural technician in Lonkam.

I threw my gear together in a hurry, said goodbye to all my friends in Milltown and took the bus to Kansas City. It still seems kind of strange leaving my farm in Kansas to take an unknown job halfway around the world. But I volunteered, and I'm thrilled by the prospects ahead.

After a couple of days of orientation, I headed for San Francisco. You might call 'Frisco the gateway between East and West: Chinatown, the old Spanish Mission Dolores, and the tall modern office buildings all blend in crazy-quilt fashion into a wonderful city.

From there we went to Honolulu, and spent a couple of days surf-riding and crammed in some more orientation. Then on to Tokyo, that half-Westernized pearl of the East. As tourists, we heard the old story of the American woman who, when asked how she liked Tokyo, answered, "I don't really know. I went

90

down to the Ginza once, but there were too many Japanese around." That takes the cake!

Our final stopover was Hong Kong. John Gordon, our chief-of-party, and his wife gave me a guided tour of the city. I ran through quite a few dollars in the process, this being the bargain capital of the world. But all of us felt guilty when we stared into the vacant faces of hungry refugees from Red China. Each day brings more of these pitiful people to this already overflowing tinderbox. Once-stout peasants from the southern provinces stand begging in the streets, rags clinging to their bones. The shacks, tenements and harbor junks that refugee families "live" in would arouse the most stonehearted of New York slum lords to reform.

By sunset we were heading back, weary and footsore, to our hotel, and then we sat around a pot of coffee and talked into the night of our experiences.

Transportation from Hong Kong to Lonkam is none too good. The plane we boarded early the next morning must have been a relic of one of Chennault's "Flying Tigers," and one passenger had a fit every time we hit an air pocket. None of us had any regrets when we stepped once again on the terra firma of Ba-Vienh, Lonkam's capital.

So here I am. In some ways now I almost feel like a veteran, but I know I am the rankest of novices. It was several months ago that I began ransacking libraries at home for information on the tiny republic of Lonkam, located in Southeast Asia. Information was hard to find, but slowly it accumulated by bits and pieces. Now more than a month after leaving the States, I'm finding it almost as hard to find out how the Lonkamese mind works. Equally so is the task

91

of dealing with the problems that arise in trying to bring modern techniques to an ancient nation whose customs are so different from ours. These are perhaps our greatest obstacles.

We've already run into a real juggernaut stemming from Lonkamese social customs. People here who are educated to any extent lose face if they do any work with their hands. On the other hand, it is nigh impossible for a man who works with his hands to get an education, regardless of his ability or talent. We need Lonkamese who are smart, who have some education, and who are willing to use their muscles.

Our two Lonkamese counterparts are very reluctant to discard hidebound norms enough to work side by side with us in manual tasks. How they expect to teach their countrymen how to assemble a plow, run an arc welder or stretch a fence, when they cannot bring themselves to dirty their hands to learn, is beyond me! If we do nothing more than put a slight dent in this crippling social custom during our time here, our mission will not have failed. Yet I cannot help but think that there must be many intelligent, dedicated young Lonkamese who see the need to combine intellect with practical application—to stoop to conquer.

Here in Ba-Vienh the afternoon rains seem good to anyone who knows the droughts of our Midwest. This is the monsoon season. During this four-month period, nearly all of the annual precipitation is received —and that is over a hundred inches. A few days ago I went shopping without an umbrella. That was a mistake. With one along I could have walked home carrying the groceries—if I had rolled up my pants legs and carried my shoes at the same time. As it was, I took a bicycle taxi, called a *cyclo* here. It was slow but fun, like boating upstream. In many of the down-town "streets" the rainwater was up to the hubs of the bicycle wheels.

All in our team are from the Midwest or the South, and we have solid farming backgrounds. Three of us had our own farms and plan to return to them. This farm experience is a vital foundation for the work we're doing, and the degree I earned at Kansas State Agricultural College has come in handy as well. One reason we're here is our know-how of machinery, motors, crops and soils. But more important is the American willingness to work—a needed influence in a small Asian nation.

USOM (U. S. Operations Mission) has loaned our party quarters here in Ba-Vienh which we'll use while in the city for business or pleasure. Just when we'll get set up in the country we don't know yet. It looks like it will be Nam-Loq, a mountain town about fifty miles from here. We've already done some "roughing it" at a couple of camps, but it is nothing like when we can set up our own station.

Today being Sunday, we went to church. Services are held in a large air-conditioned room in the Em-bassy which doubles as theater, meeting place, school for new arrivals, and recreation center. Space is at a premium.

Every day we study spoken Lonkamese and can boast a small vocabulary now. We can tell time, give directions, count, order a meal, and carry on a half-way decent coversation. Our tortured efforts are not wasted—Lonkamese are always telling us how im-pressed they are that rich Americans (*all* Americans are Rockefellers, we're assured) would take the trou-ble to learn their language.

Back in the States, you seldom got more than two lines out of me, but being in the boondocks has changed all that. Letters won't be too frequent, though, with so much to do and learn here. So long for now.

ANDY

*Nam-Loq, Lonkam*
*November 2, 1959*

DEAR FOLKS,

As I write this letter I'm sitting on a tree stump in our new camp. A foggy mist has hidden the neighboring peaks of the Rhadmer mountain range, and the sun shimmers through in quiet desperation.

For someone who enjoys the rugged life outdoors, this place is Utopia. Walking down a jungle bullock-cart road, machete in hand and a rifle slung over one shoulder, is just about the most enjoyable experience I've found yet. You can't see very far, but the forest sounds are there, and if you stop and really tune in, they can tell you a lot.

For the past few weeks we've been busy hacking away at the jungle, clearing a site for our temporary headquarters. Three pole-frame buildings, with thatched roofs and walls, have been built so far. Two of the largest are to serve as living quarters for the workers, and a small one will serve as an office of sorts.

Our own living quarters are rather unique. We have two large "covered wagons" in which we sleep on canvas cots covered with mosquito nets. Next to the wagons is a medical truck, complete with water-storage tanks, cupboards and an electric generator. Lonkam's Veterinary Service loaned it to us temporarily since it wasn't in use. Covering the whole arrangement is a thatched roof supported by a pole frame. And we have adequate pots and pans, dishes and utensils. For some time we had to make do with an old kerosene stove, but one of the worker's wives kept borrowing it and neglected to return it. So USOM recently contributed an old gas stove with an oven and a couple of bottles of gas. Our refrigerator is a hole in the ground in which we put a couple of ice chunks brought from nearby Nam-Loq. In short, all the comforts of home (well, almost).

A better setup is planned, but this will have to do for the time being. We'll soon have to erect a makeshift shower. Until now, everyone has been bathing in the river. It's so muddy, though, that you have doubts whether the dirt is washed off, rearranged or just exchanged for more. The workers are no help at all in this respect. One of their practical jokers has been spreading rumors that a large crocodile occasionally visits our bathing area. Since we can't tell if this is just pure fantasy or some truth with the usual Lonkamese exaggeration, no one enters the water without getting jittery.

Working in the jungle is no unmixed pleasure, either. We have to wear clothing that protects our legs and feet from brambles, possible snakebite, and leeches. (The shorts worn in Hollywood movie scenes are only practical in clearings.) Leeches are a bloodsucker type of varmint found all over during the rainy season. Attaching themselves to your skin (legs and ankles mostly), they proceed to freeload on your blood to the bursting point, then drop off. The trouble is you ordinarily don't realize any of this until you look down at your bloodsoaked pants or your boots start squishing. The ungrateful leech has an anti-coagulant effect, so the blood keeps flowing freely even after he's had his fill. This is dangerous only if large numbers of leeches join your little friend for lunch, or if the bite gets infected. It does seem a waste of good American blood, so we learn to tie our pants legs snugly and check occasionally.

The native workers we employ are a happy and carefree lot. They have few worldly possessions, but apparently they're happy so long as they have a job, a roof over their heads, and ample food. Some are Moslem, others are Buddhist, and a minority are Confucianist. At one time, these groups formed distinct ethnic units because of their national origins, but the mixing of the races down through the years has made them practically indistinguishable in all but religion.

The personal friendships we are forming with the Lonkamese may be one important aspect of our work. They are finding that IVS team members are working people whose main interest is the projects underway. Living near the workers, taking the time necessary to help them learn new techniques, in turn learning some of their language and their ways of life, and in this way earning their respect as well as their friendship—these things we must and will do.

Of course, we neither pretend nor want to become integrated into Lonkamese society. Of necessity we are set apart from them—largely because of our different standards of living. But this can work to an advantage. Our tools and conveniences, few though they are in the field, are luxuries to the local people, and they attract their attention and fascination. This gives us a chance to apply a little basic mechanical education for the interested and ambitious ones.

By its very nature, our work is slow: success may come slowly, or even go unnoticed. Frankly, mistakes will be common and the alternative courses of action many. Because Nam-Loq Agricultural Station belongs to Lonkam's government, we, as part of the U. S. co-operative assistance program, must assume a backstairs role—not intruding, but rather willing to help where help is asked. Sure, we get discouraged sometimes—and confused. It's no easy matter to adjust to the shock of a new culture, to have all your old ground swept right from under you. But we feel this type of grass-roots, person-to-person effort is both vital and desirable. Our small-scale projects, coupled with the huge enterprises ICA has undertaken, can help to accelerate economic growth and to raise the living standards and human dignity of the individual Lonkamese as well.

We've heard rumors recently that Communist-supported guerrillas are pushing south, and we may hear from them yet. Repeated efforts by the central government to dislodge them from their mountain strongholds have largely been unsuccessful. Small wonder—that vast, uncharted jungle gives rebels (and bandits) ideal cover for strike-and-retreat operations, and after ten years in that maze, those boys are real experts in the arts of survival.

What do we do for entertainment out here, you ask. Well, the Lonkamese workers sit around campfires and tell tall tales on through the night. We don't understand much Lonkamese yet, but from the loud guffaws we hear, they must be humdingers. And every Wednesday night USOM supplies us with a couple of Lonkamese-language films. No English subtitles, but most of the films are travelogs and newsreels, and the scenery is often breathtaking. Have you ever seen the majestic waterfalls and rapids of Southeast Asia or the inside of ancient jeweled temples? And other films have featured the growth of the American Union. For many Lonkamese, these are the first movies they've ever seen, and they come for miles around. Incidentally, the spirit of free enterprise is no U. S. prerogative—the local women have a pretty good racket working on movie nights. These sharp operators bring in fruits, meats, and cooked rice to sell to the crowds at a nice profit.

Last week I got a touch of dysentery; I'm still a little woozy but otherwise okay. Our only accident happened about two weeks ago when a local counterpart, Dao Nonkin, was burned rather badly while lighting a pile of stumps and refuse. He's in the hospital at Ba-Vienh, but the way he's recuperating, he should be back on the job next month. He lost his eyebrows and eyelashes, and the skin on his face still looks raw, but the medic says it'll all heal up.

It's a damn good feeling to know that the French hospital in Ba-Vienh is good, both in facilities and staff. If need be, the USOM planes can fly seriously injured or sick persons at a moment's notice to the big hospital in Bangkok (Thailand). We have a dry landing strip at Nam-Loq, and USOM is going to install a telephone for use in emergencies.

Last night we had a real bull session via interpreter with our Lonkamese co-workers, and questions mostly concerned—yep, you guessed it—Little Rock, the Cuban revolution, our two-party system, and the Cold War. Here the clash of ideologies is close to home, and there's no escaping it. We often meet Russian technicians and Chinese exchange students on the streets of Ba-Vienh, and sometimes out in the jungle country. Oh, they're very correct and polite, but there's no love lost. You realize increasingly you're being watched very closely, and your conduct is under strict scrutiny all the time. If you don't watch your P's and Q's, brother, you've had it. The fewer "ugly Americans" we get out here, the better.

Well, take it easy, and drop me a line once in a while.

ANDY

*Nam-Loq, Lonkam*
*December 28, 1959*

DEAR FOLKS,

All your letters have now arrived. Such a wealth of news I've never seen: marriages and births appear the sole occupation of Kansans. If there is any single woman around, you might do me the favor of locking her in a cage until I return, because at this rate there won't be one left for at least the next couple of generations.

The life here, though never quite humdrum, is more natural to me now. I've found it is far easier to adapt the body to changes than it is the mind. My bony frame will readily welcome the hardest rock as a Simmons mattress, but making my mind go along is a different matter. The secret to meeting these difficulties is making mind and body achieve a balance in regard to all the aspects of the problem. Once you do that, you're okay. I admit that at the beginning I kind of worried whether or not I'd meet the re-

99

quirements—now I laugh when I think of these early apprehensions.

We've learned that to get the work done around here you've got to work hand-in-hand with the people—it can't be any sham where the Americans walk in and take over, leaving the natives a few empty titles. My efforts with the Dalat tribes show this. The Dalat are hillbillies who live much the same as American Indians in the frontier days.

About two months ago the Communists started pressuring the mountaineers into coming over to their side. The main basis for their campaign was that the government and the American "interlopers" had done nothing but give phony promises to "better the lot" of the Dalat. Sadly enough this was true in some instances, and the Communists were making headway in most tribal areas.

At the same time the Reds were pushing their effort, IVS/Nam-Loq was using every possible means to establish a basis of mutual trust with the Dalat. Meetings were organized with village leaders to discuss problems and the ways to solve them. Meanwhile, we contacted Lonkamese officials who might be of assistance if some means were found to offer a solution to the Dalat's problems.

However, a quick source of money had to be found. Our need was now, and confidence would have been lost had we been forced to wait on the usual "red-tape" government channels. But we were lucky in this case, as we got some funds right away from a private aid foundation.

A committee of Dalat representatives discussed with us the chances for an agricultural training school to learn techniques to better their lot. Lonkam's Minister of Agriculture promised full co-operation and the aid foundation approved our project on the spot. It was only a matter of days before the school was organized and in session. Arrangements were made for practical assistance such as seeds and plows. If projects like these can be carried out, they may be the very thing to keep Lonkam independent and free. Not so meaningful to the ordinary Lonkamese are the big money programs written up on paper to take place one or two years from now.

We had a visit the other day from USOM forester Jack Clark and a crew of laborers. They're surveying the jungles of the Rhadmer mountain ranges. The area is a large one. First you travel by jeep, then by ox-cart, and finally by foot, often in places where no man has ever trod. There's one advantage, though: you automatically have a hunting trip at the same time.

Speaking of hunting, the local villagers are always warning us of the "Tiger Phantom." The legend goes like this. A hunter builds his perch in a tree near an animal that the tiger has killed and partly eaten. He sits there with his rifle and waits for the tiger to return for another meal. But the tiger is too smart. Realizing its foe is waiting to pounce, it takes the form of a most beautiful and seductive woman. "She" then lures the hunter from the tree for a *tête-à-tête*. Once he is on the ground, the phantom immediately changes back into a tiger and devours the hunter. The area abounds in rich folklore like this.

Mr. Noffsinger in Washington was right when he warned us that we would need three indispensable things for success: patience, more patience, and still more patience. Nam-Loq's main occupation now is waiting—waiting for the local people to be paid for the land they have cleared so we can make it into fields, then prepare it for planting crops at the beginning of the rainy season; waiting for the road from the highway to the farm to be rebuilt, so that materials may be hauled in and out; waiting for permanent buildings to be built so that all of us—IVS staff, the Lonkamese counterparts, the equipment, and the livestock—will have suitable housing. And, of course, these are all major items which will be "started any day now" for the last month and more, that is, according to those responsible for getting the projects underway.

The river, translated, is called "the river which runs backwards," and now it's flowing toward the ocean like a good river should. I was a mite skeptical when I first arrived here when they told me it ran one way in the rainy season, then another during the dry season. The change in this ornery river has convinced me, though—the water level has varied by as much as thirty feet from one season to the next.

Our native interpreter is also a professional fisherman. So he is leading the workers in construction of a fish trap. It stretches across the river to a point just above our swimming hole. We hope it will furnish enough fish for everybody. The trap, made of bamboo and vine, is designed to catch all of the larger fish which attempt to travel through it. The Lonkamese have warned our Chinese-born Izaak Walton that such a large-scale project could cause him bad luck with the river spirits. Maybe they regard such thorough-going fish traps as too greedy?

People in America can never realize the conditions that many people in Southeast Asia must endure.

102

What is astounding is their attitude. Normal conditions at their best would be very uncomfortable for us, and at their worst a catastrophe. We live under the relative security of a strong government and a comfortably high standard of living; here the only government they understand is the village chief, and routine existence is plodding behind a water buffalo pulling a wooden plow in a soggy rice paddy. A robbery in the neighborhood is horrible to Americans; to Lonkamese this is nothing. The Red guerrillas attack their villages and then tell the survivors to pay their meager year's foodstores as tribute. The next thing they know the central government is on their backs with penalties for "collaborating" with the rebels.

Coexistence with tragedy and continual disquiet is the philosophy. One of the workers lost a month's wages and some clothing to a thief recently. I heard about it and went to console him, expecting to find him downcast and sullen. Instead, he was working furiously and smiled to me in greeting. When I asked him about his loss, he merely shrugged. "It could have been worse," he said. "Three days ago I had six months' pay saved, which I used to buy a rice paddy and that healthy buffalo you see over there. I'm glad the thief didn't rob me then." This looking at the bright side of things is a trait I envy. It's a native asset we couldn't do without in trying to do the impossible out here.

Otherwise, the weather has been dandy. We've forgotten what the long hard winters back in the States are like. Right now it's 92° F. in the shade. I felt kind of silly singing "Jingle Bells" Christmas Eve when it was like a day in mid-June.

ANDY

*Nam-Loq, Lonkam*
*February 10, 1960*

DEAR FOLKS,

The last few weeks have been eventful ones for us, beginning with the National Agricultural Exposition in Ba-Vienh. IVS played only a small part, primarily in preparing some of the Lonkamese Veterinary Service displays. Dr. Pham Ngao of the Service was overall chairman of the fair, and Bill Pearce, our USOM advisor, gave us a great deal of assistance.

The Chinese Communists attracted a lot of attention with their textile loom, operating almost continuously throughout. Models of the textile mill, paper plant and cement factory—all completed and working—were large and appeared well laid out and equipped. Two of their industrial plants are near Nam-Loq, and, together with the large modern Russian-built hospital in Ba-Vienh, make an impressive showcase of Communist aid in this area.

With complete modesty, however, we can say that the Veterinary Service display was the biggest hit of the fair. Peasants and foreign envoys alike craned their necks to see our exhibit: an incubator in which baby chicks were hatching. There were startled cries of glee as little bundles of fuzz began to pop out of their shells. In addition, Dao Nonkin, a Lonkamese counterpart, helped prepare a scale model of the livestock-development farm on which we are working; he set up buildings, fences, green grass and even cattle in the pastures. The farm model looked fine, and with the southern end of the mountain range for backdrop, the real thing should look even better.

IVS/Nam-Loq has undergone something of a revolution since my last letter. Enough progress has been made so that the remaining work of getting established can be laid out and checked off, item by item. Essentially all the temporary hourly workers have been laid off and sent to help other projects. All future work will be by contract. We hope to get more done for your money by paying for work *done,* instead of for the number of hours put in.

The right-of-way is being widened and cleared along the road from the highway to the farm. It is to be hard surfaced all the way in. The first few parts near the highway have been built up and prepared for surfacing, but the rainy season has arrived and the roadwork is only beginning.

Work in the plant nursery so far indicates that several local grasses will do well here. Also, millets, cowpeas, sorghums, legumes, and grasses from the southern part of the U. S. have done well during the dry season under irrigation. What they will do during the rainy season remains to be seen. The soil here is not fertile, even that which has never been farmed. Apparently the heat and the heavy rainfall decompose and leach organic matter and minerals from the soil at a very rapid rate.

The other day we were working out in the hot midday sun, and thought we would stop for lunch. That had to be postponed, however, while the mountain folk gathered around to stare unabashed at us newcomers, especially at the white woman (John Gordon's wife). This sport of staring is widespread all over Asia and just about everybody but the most sheltered prude gets a kick out of it. These people don't see too much of strangers, so after a while you get a little used to it. To sort of clear the air, we gave out with our best "hellos" in Lonkamese, though I'm sure they got an even bigger kick out of that.

Land clearing is progressing. All sorts of vegetables have been added to our diet: onions, radishes, cabbage, okra, and sweet corn. Six bulls have arrived from the States, and we've taught the farm hands how to teach them to lead and how to care for them. Another stroke of luck: USOM gave us a dilapidated but still quite workable station wagon for the long trips we must make. Hundreds of loads of sand have been hauled past our camp by trucks from the Red Chinese-built cement plant nearby.

Dao Nonkin has been in charge of surveying the 120 hectares that we'll have as extra pasture and crop land. Many trees, brush piles, and termite mounds have combined with intense heat to make progress slow. Still, more than half the area is surveyed now and drainage ditches can be located properly.

Our experimental plantings of Kenaf, a fiber crop, are the first in this area. We have hopes that it will be a new cash crop for the farmers here. By the way, the expanding industrialization of Japan is providing quite a market for fiber crops in the Far East.

The well has been completed and is functioning right. But it appears that we will have quite a time convincing the workers that they should not take baths, wash their clothes and dishes, etc., right at the pump. They are used to using water wherever they find it and see no harm in using all the water right at the pump where it's handy. No doubt they think we're nuts for insisting that they take their baths elsewhere.

Our project has at last passed through the embryonic stage successfully and is now on its feet. It's growing pretty fast. It shouldn't be too many months before we start "phasing out" and leave Nam-Loq in the hands of the natives we've worked with and trained. It's a weird feeling to work yourself out of a job—and then have to like it, too. But that's our mission.

ANDY

# CHAPTER 2

# CRS/HONAI (VIETNAM)

Catholic Relief Services, an agency of the National
Catholic Welfare Conference, has been operating
assistance programs since the late thirties, when it
began resettling refugees from Nazi Germany. Since
that time, CRS activities have expanded to many
times its original effort.

The Peace Corps does not anticipate any health
projects using skilled medical technicians during its
first year of operation; instead, it will start with public
health units designed to teach sanitation and to apply
minor medical care. Still, the following CRS case
history is doubly important: in the first place, the
Honai eye clinic was very similar in circumstances
and purpose to Dr. Tom Dooley's work in Laos.
Secondly, it is an example of how the facilities and
resources of a religious group can be used effectively
and without the slightest hint of proselytizing.

Beginning in 1954, 900,000 Vietnamese "voted with
their feet"—to use a pet expression of Vladimir Ilyich
Lenin—in an election that had far-reaching conse-
quences. The demigod of Communism would have

been heartsick to see these men, women, and children fleeing his disciples' "People's Democracy" in North Vietnam for life in the bourgeois South.

The mass exodus conferred problems as well as a boon on South Vietnam. Many of the refugees were disease-ridden, and the war-torn nation had few facilities and still fewer personnel to handle even the most serious cases.

The most crippling of all is trachoma, the greatest single chronic eye problem in the country. In trachoma, the eyelids become deformed in such a way that the eyelashes scratch the cornea each time the individual opens or closes his eyes. It is not hard to see why it is painful, ultimately blinding and economically disastrous. Yet it can be cleared away in the early stages with simple drug treatment; in advanced cases, a minor operation will suffice. Trachoma victims can be rehabilitated in a matter of a week or so, as compared to the years-long treatment required for such Asian commonplaces as leprosy and tuberculosis.

Nearly as common are such eye afflictions as glaucoma, both local and virulent tumors, ulcer of the cornea, crossed eyes, and the ordinary "pink eye." The trouble is that there are not more than nine eye specialists to care for the approximately 12 million Vietnamese.

In 1959, a concerned Hawaiian ophthalmologist, Dr. William Holmes, asked Catholic Relief Services to give an eye clinic project a trial run in South Vietnam. Monsignor Joseph J. Harnett agreed to sponsor it, and Dr. Holmes scouted around for qualified volunteers.

The site chosen was Honai, thirty kilometers from

the capital Saigon. The Canadian nursing Brothers of St. John of God, themselves refugees from the North, staff a hospital there. American pharmaceutical companies and volunteer groups donated special medicines, drugs and equipment, while the German Bishops' Overseas Relief (MISEREOR) provided an X-ray laboratory. All these materials were shipped by CRS under the ICA ocean freight subsidy and were allowed duty-free entry by the South Vietnam government.

The volunteer eye specialists paid out of their own pockets for the transportation to and from Saigon. And for the duration of the project, they sacrificed their private practice back home. CRS provided the doctors with housing, board and transportation within Vietnam.

The makeshift character of the Honai clinic is emphasized by the fact that operating-room linens and surgical gowns were improvised from discarded surplus flour sacks and odd scraps of cloth. Used glasses were obtained from "Eyes for the Needy," an American organization; the greatest use of these was for those who have difficulty in using their eyes for near work.

By February, 1960, the project was off and running. The first ophthalmologist to report for duty was Dr. Eliot B. Hague of Buffalo, New York, who brought along his wife, a registered nurse experienced in eye work. After him came Dr. Jou S. Tchao of Lewiston, Maine, and Dr. Herman A. Iverson of Eureka, California. All were Protestants. Assisting the doctors were Brother Bernard Samuel and Mrs. Catherine Varella, a CRS registered nurse, plus the native staff of trainees.

Although the clinic was not advertised in the local newspapers, word-of-mouth and immediate results brought an onrush of would-be patients. Many traveled by foot from as far away as the town of Hué, 690 miles to the northeast. For this reason, inpatient facilities had to be enlarged several times, and when space ran out, patients were packed in the already-crowded wards. Patients able to take care of themselves were put in one big ward. At one time as many as 34 eye cases were cared for in one day at the hospital.

In the operating room, standards were made as close to Stateside hospitals as possible. What would have meant extra cost was accomplished through a lot of extra effort and longer hours. Scarcity of things that could not have been done without elsewhere would have created the same problem at Honai except that Asians toughened by hard life offered an incredibly high resistance to pain and suffering. Many patients went through as painful a procedure as the removal of an eye with only a small dose of local anesthetic, gritting of teeth, and, as one remarked wryly, "much prayer." In the four months that the clinic was in operation, surgery on 389 cases was completed. Many more could have been operated on if another surgeon had been there to assume post-operative care and follow-up.

More than eye troubles were cured. Trachoma and similar diseases work havoc on human dignity. Unable to work or to lead a normal life, the victim often becomes morose, his spirits take a nosedive and his physical bearing is stooped. One young woman patient had been blind for twelve years. She had lost her right eye, and her left one had begun to fade away. Her daughter led her to the clinic, as she could not walk by herself. The operation was successful, and when her daughter returned to help her, she refused and walked unaided and standing straight, enjoying her newly regained self-reliance.

Of the thousands who came, a large number of all but the most serious cases had to be turned away. Even so, approximately 3,000 were examined and treated. The harassed doctors were, therefore, quick to see the need for an educational campaign to prevent or reduce advanced cases. Aside from the shortage of personnel, ignorance and reluctance to see a doctor cause most of the eye trouble in Vietnam. The hospital staff hung crudely drawn pictures on the walls, and attached some explanations in Vietnamese. Madison Avenue admen are not likely to award the effort the Advertising Council prize of the year, but it went a long way toward accomplishing its purpose. Honai was helped here to a large degree by native medical authorities; Dr. Nguyen-Dinh-Cat, chairman of the Saigon University Medical School, supplemented their efforts by lectures.

One of the most pressing problems at Honai—and throughout Southeast Asia—was lack of qualified nurses and interns. The eye clinic tried to "steal" some help from the hospital, but they were so shorthanded that none could be spared. The lucrative fees that American medical technicians command make service in a project of this sort no small sacrifice, and it was recommended that CRS recruit personnel instead from Japan or Germany.

All reports to CRS have emphasized that the clinic should be put on a more permanent basis. But it is only during the four or five months of the dry season, from December to May, that work can be practical. In the monsoon, rice fields and harvesting occupy the undivided attention of the Vietnamese farmers; the rainy season imposes additional hardships on the needy and their companions who have to travel miles over the countryside to reach the hospital.

However, the Peace Corps feels that a permanently staffed hospital is out of their line. Realizing this, CRS has suggested instead a mobile unit which would operate throughout the area and close down when work became impractical or need not so immediate. How this might be arranged within the scope of the Peace Corps is not known at present, but both the ICA and Corpsmen have expressed sympathy for it; after a recent trip through Asia, a top administration official put Honai and similar projects on the foreign aid priority list. Despite this seeming discord, all are agreed that a concerted effort must be made to improve the abysmal health conditions of the Asian peasant.

# CHAPTER 3

# DIARY OF A CROSSROADER
# (NIGERIA)

The people belong to the Ijaw tribe. Unfortunately, due to their geographical location in the Niger delta, they have suffered from lack of education, electricity, roads, good water, etc. The death rate is appalling. I talked with three local fishermen —two had six wives each: the first had five children surviving out of twenty, the second only seven out of twenty-three. . . . Plural marriages are almost a necessity if the average man has any hope of raising a normal-sized family. . . .

During a tour of Africa in 1954, Dr. James H. Robinson, a Negro pastor in Harlem, saw conditions worse than these and came back to the United States determined to do something about it. At first, he might as well have been talking to the moon, for many people thought he had lost his senses. Finally, though, students at Occidental College in Los Angeles and at other universities agreed to work with him in setting up work camps in Africa, and church and civic groups financed the project. Out of 270 applications, sixty students were chosen as the first group to represent

114

the new "Operation Crossroads-Africa" during the summer of 1958. They were then divided into five projects, to serve six weeks each in French Cameroun, Ghana, Liberia, Nigeria, and Sierra Leone.

Since that time, Crossroads has become an enterprise of 180 young men and women, representing 100 colleges across the country and just about every religion and race. The work accomplished prompted the first Assistant Secretary of State for African Affairs, Joseph C. Satterthwaite, to call it "one of the most successful ventures that American private citizens have ever undertaken in Africa south of the Sahara." Further recognition was accorded Crossroads when President Kennedy named Dr. Robinson as one of four vice-chairmen on the Peace Corps Advisory Council. Oddly enough, however, its short-term projects put Crossroads outside the plans of the Peace Corps. Both sides, on the other hand, feel that the human and work experience gained by Crossroads will help the new government agency invaluably in hurdling obstacles in future African projects.

"Diary of a Crossroader" is authentic and has been compiled from the notes of the 1960 western Nigeria group. Whereas in "IVS/Indochina" a series of letters portrayed life in the field over a period of time, the diary gives the fresh daily impressions of a worker in the African bush.

## June 29 (Shagamu)

A week ago, our group left New York for London. A couple of days' orientation and sightseeing were then spent in London and Lagos, the capital of Nigeria. It was good, however, to get right to the work camp at Shagamu.

A rigid daily schedule was posted this morning, which I guess we'll get used to. Up at 6 A.M., then quiet time with coffee and work until breakfast at 9. Back to work until noon, 15 minutes out for a snack, then work. At 2:30 we stop working for lunch, then we have organized games, improvised entertainment, and finally supper and lights out. We're told, however, that parts of the schedule will be dropped altogether, including the A.M. quiet time and the organized games at night.

The first project chosen was a 300-yard road, to be cut through thick bush. We feel this is better than field-leveling or building in this particular locality—tools are limited anyway. The road will connect a public road on the opposite side of the campus with a future chapel.

Later in the day, students of Remo Secondary School joined us in hacking away at the bush. They were excited over university students working alongside them. Our girl participants were most popular, especially if they showed the time-honored signs of hard toil, dirt and sweat.

*June 30*

The second day of work brought even greater energies from both participants and Remo students. A British school instructor, Mr. Jones, joined his pupils, much to their delight. One wonders if the Englishman's sweat and the joyful young African are two strokes of the pen which will write a strange new page in colonial history. Passing Nigerians were heard to comment laughingly, "My, the world is certainly changing! Those are the first whites who ever used axes and worked with us."

116

Our evening discussion was conducted informally by two Americans and two Nigerians as panelists in a debate on segregation in the United States and South Africa. It was pointed out that American racial policy was based upon progressive integration supported by law, whereas South Africa's *apartheid* is the exact opposite.

Supper was taken at the home of Tai Solarin, headmaster of Mayflower School in Ikenne and former member of Nigeria's House of Representatives. Here we learned by the meal served us how patient our Nigerian counterparts had been with the non-peppered dishes we prepared. One of our girls, however, drew the line when it came to cooked rooster head and had to relinquish it to Olajide, a Nigerian student.

## July 3

Anglican and Methodist church services were attended in Shagamu; Crossroaders were introduced to the congregations by the ministers. In the Methodist church, every seat was taken. The old men sat in the front, praying and reading Scripture, while a swallow flew in the window and made the rounds of the sanctuary. When it had had enough of our company, the bird flew back out the window, and a hesitant lizard scaling the doorway engaged my attention. A Nigerian tapped me on the shoulder to tell me that a certain part in the Yuraba dialect service was for our group.

Our Sunday go-meeting clothes donned, we went to visit the Paramount Chief, Oba M.S. Owolesi Erinwole II, in his palace. The Oba is council chairman over fifteen other village chiefs in the Remo area. He took his turn after two other official dynasties in 1952

117

and can be replaced only at death. He proudly announced that he was a Christian of the Methodist Church, despite the six wives he has. A group leader asked him how he could reconcile his polygamy with his Christianity, and he came off with what I thought was a new slant on things. "If you are a minister of religion, you will have only one wife. But if I can not belong as a layman with my six wives, then I will go to another church. If I take one wife to church, she contributes to the collection. If I take six, they all contribute and the church is the better off for it—Why should they complain? The chief before me had thirty wives, yet he was a Christian, also."

## July 4

Morning assembly at Remo School was given over to American participants for an Independence Day program. We had a salute to Old Glory, the "Star-Spangled Banner" was sung, read a portion of our Declaration of Independence and closed with "America." Two of us spoke and answered questions in three history classes during the day, then asked Remo students to write essays on their impressions of this and of the Crossroads project.

Later, we had a discussion of the political problems of soon-to-be independent Nigeria, and identified the struggles of our Revolution with theirs. Four main obstacles to progress in Nigeria, students told us, are illiteracy, the language barrier, communications and trade, and tribal traditionalism. In the north, the main political party is the Northern People's Congress, led by the Premier, the Sarduna of Sokoto. It is opposed by the young westernized politicians of the Northern Elements Progressive Union. The action group led by Awolowa of the Western Region and Azikiwe's National Council of Nigeria and the Cameroons in the Eastern Region complete the list of strong parties in the country.

## July 8

A series of three work projects has been undertaken in nearby areas in an attempt to work with the townspeople and increase the aim of the work camp. Mr. Aladejo Akinosun, head of the Vountary Work Camps Association, made the arrangements. More than half of us joined nearly 200 men, representing the trade and semi-skilled workers of Shagamu, in a road project north of town.

Others chose the day to observe the National Nigerian Student Convention, and three participants conducted a worship service at Shagamu's Methodist church that evening. Only a little distance across town, though, a less peaceful event occurred—clashes between political factions broke out and seven men were charged with the murder of four others.

## July 10

The group returned to the Remo Road project today. The main activity centers on leveling the road, but progress is slow because of insufficient tools. A girl participant received instructions and cheers from dozens of the Nigerian men, and this inspired a few of the passing Nigerian women to work with us.

Certain of the Nigerian university students working with us are inspiring as they express their role in their emergent nation's future. "We must end man's inhumanity to man on the African continent . . . we must give convincing proof of well-disciplined minds

119

that can rise above party jealousies and unhealthy tribal rivalries." They feel that they will be traitors to Nigeria if they fail to direct their accumulated knowledge to the service of their people. We, for our part, must recognize that these Nigerians will manage their own affairs and shape their nation's history—the role of the Briton, American or Russian is to stand ready to assist whenever asked, and not before.

The evening talk was on dating, courtship, and marriage in Nigeria and the United States. We learned that the two traditions are so different that comparisons are difficult to make. The present generation of Yuraba youth is experiencing and initiating changes in their marriage traditions. One wonders just how valuable some African traditions might be to Western society. In Africa, a man is bound by law to support each child for which he is responsible. In America, such a man boldly forces, by his silence, his society to pay for his behavior.

### July 15

Several of our group spent the day touring a nearby village. A Remo student was guide, yet the villagers were slow in warming to photos and conversation— It turned out that they were afraid our group was surveying their property and would create tension and strife with other villages.

Another bunch of participants joined another community development project, and, as in Shagamu, townspeople and students pitched in earnestly to help.

Work was extended into the afternoon hours so that 180 Shagamu Boy Scouts could take a few licks at the bush. These kids are well mannered and bubbling with enthusiasm.

120

## July 16

Rain prevented work on the road during the morning hours, so we split up to visit the local hospital and conduct group discussions for 250 students at the nearby Muslim high school. Meanwhile, our group leader returned to tell us that arrangements were now complete to start a work-camp project at the small town of Akugbene, 27 miles away by riverboat from Warri.

The debate this evening quickened some tempers. It was on British policy in Nigeria. One Nigerian student complained that it "turned out to be a defense of the white man's club against Nigerian assault. Whenever a Nigerian posed a question on problems, some American would jump in to say America has the same problem—as if Nigeria must have it since America does." We could have done with more accurate and honest observation from both sides. Mr. Jones, the moderator, is respected by all and is a veritable encyclopedia, yet there were times when he seemed like an apologetic straggler in the wake of departed British colonialism as he tried to rationalize the contradictions in colonial history.

## July 17

Today, men participants attended a fetish worship in Ilishan. Cameras were dangerous baggage to have along. We came away convinced that the event was named accurately—pure and simple fetish worship.

## July 20

Tempers flared again when a *Time* Magazine article about Crossroaders in Nigeria was read at the evening meal. Nigerians took offense at *Time*'s characterizations and patronizing slant. The whole project came close to disruption, as it was thought that someone in our group had written it— It turned out later, however, that it was a staff rewrite of *Time*'s correspondent in Lagos. American participants were divided in their reaction—some were defensive about *Time* Magazine itself, while others were angry that the Nigerians could get "so stupid about some little ole newspaper article."

But the Nigerians had little patience with that sort of reasoning. One Nigerian student retorted that, thanks to the slanted U. S. press, "the average American still thinks of Nigerians as wearing animal skins and unintelligible." Even a prominent American evangelist, he continued, said recently that human meat is still sold in the market, by way of contrasting a benighted, pagan Nigeria with the enlightened, God-fearing United States.

"*Time*," another said, "bemoaned the fact that these 'fifteen fresh-faced American college students' should be 'stifling in Nigeria's rainy-season heat.' The students are probably stifling in our heat but if they wanted to stay fresh and have a rollicking time, they have chosen the wrong place. Crossroaders expected worse than they have got and are happily reconciled to our climate. This incident is so trivial when compared to a project like Operation Crossroads, but the degradation and persecution of Nigeria by the U. S. press is galling."

As Nigerian anger was directed at *Time* and American publishers, it was pointed out that a moment's glance reveals a Nigerian newspaper's political party alignment—each prints open slander against personalities of the opposition. A Nigerian writer described the Nigerian press as "a weapon [under which] you boil, you fume, you fret, you spit, you sweat, you swear, you roast in the heat of your own indignation. . . ." [1] The hurt ingrained deep inside the young Nigerians made such protests superfluous, and their minds were already made up.

We've learned a lot from this experience, and the matter is now settled, thanks to willingness by many persons to go more than halfway.

## July 21

Our group this morning heard a farewell speech by Nigerian student leader Dejo Akinosun, thanking Crossroaders for the road project and for insight into the principles of the work camp.

Later, we moved on to Mayflower School six miles away at Ikenne. We were housed in a newly constructed home intended for an American couple who planned to teach Mayflower students. Everybody was assigned various work projects according to preference and experience. Some installed Florida-type Venetian blinds in the house, while others wired, cleared roads, dug dirt, placed poles, strung power lines, or cooked.

## July 25

An early-morning bus trip was made toward the town of Jebba on the river Niger in Northern Nigeria. We walked across bridges, hillsides, and through the town—seeing the sights, meeting the townsmen, and viewing the centuries-old brass statues there.

[1] Tai Solarin, *Toward Nigeria's Moral Self-Government* (Ibadan, Nigeria: Ibadan University Press, 1959).

Later in the day, we visited the Oba of Benin, Akenzua II, who showed us around Benin City, its woodcarving centers, museums, and the 14th century moat that surrounded the town. Afterwards, 400 Nigerians greeted us at the local conference hall, where we danced, sang and debated until late.

*July 30*

At 8:30 this morning a fifty-foot government launch took us to Akugbene. Narrow dugout canoes slid by with native pilots perched high in the stern. Trees leaned out over swampy shores with their white roots extended high above the water as if standing tiptoe to avoid getting wet. As we inched near the village of Akugbene, gun salutes were heard and standing on the shore, cheering and waving, were somber chiefs, students dressed in white, and dozens of naked children.

After the formal ceremonies of greeting, we headed for our quarters—the girls are to live upstairs in the local post office, the boys in a newly built home. Villagers gave us mosquito nets, sheets, pillows and pillowcases, and beds. Their own homes are mud huts —open windows, mats on the floors, wood benches, no electricity or running water. We will have to depend on rains for our drinking and cooking water.

Akugbene stretches for a quarter of a mile along Forcados Creek in the Niger delta. The opposite bank is supposed to be the home of gorillas. The bush behind the town contains monkeys, leopards and tarantula spiders.

The embankment which we will help construct is to be the second half of a series of walks which have been built to retain a usable bank where the river current constantly wears the bank away. The main roadway runs along the river between the two walls.

Several of the girls visited the dispensary where they are constructing a maternity center. A midwife there said she delivers about five to eight babies a year. They use palm oil— 2–3 tablespoons to stop bleeding, then massaging to regain consciousness from eclampsia. When complications get too severe, they attempt to get a doctor. With the baby delivered and washed, the mother gets up immediately, washes herself, and from then on cares for the baby herself. Liquid quinine is given to the baby until it is thought he is immune from malaria.

*August 4*

The reinforcing wall is being constructed from cement blocks and a weak, sandy mixture of mortar. The project was divided into three parts—the village sections each assign men to help us when we are working on the portion of the wall near them. Although the men are not allowed to spend their regular amount of time fishing during our stay, they have thrown everything they have into the work and often continue working long after we quit.

The occupation of the people is determined by geographical conditions. In order of importance, they are:

Fishing—with hooks, baskets and spears. The catch is smoked and sold.
Canoes—skilled villagers carve them out of logs.
Farming—only on small scale along Niger's banks.
Distilling of native gin.
Palm-nut collecting.

In addition there are a few teachers and government officials.

Akugbene foods include yams, cocoyams, garri, fish, and various fruits which are found abundantly in the bush. A starch called *Osu* is eaten with certain soups. Other foods include groundnuts, sweet potatoes, sugar cane, beans, pepper, and grapefruit.

Five guests came to dinner—two townsmen and three Europeans who were surveying in this area for the Shell British Petroleum Company. There is great interest these days in oil, a natural resource recently discovered in the delta province area here. Right now, it is highly expensive to extract, but promises to be one of Nigeria's industries.

*August 9*

A long section of wall, laid yesterday during the group leader's absence by reason of sickness, had to be taken up and relaid at the correct level. One further hindrance is that we are running out of cement blocks, even though numerous villagers have blocks ready for use in building construction. The trouble is that we have to use every power of persuasion to get the owner of blocks to loan them to us until more blocks can be made for him. The torrential rains are no help, either, when it comes to getting the work done.

I've learned there are three types of religion here. There are Christians who believe in one God and that no other power has control over man. Then there are the faith-healers. When one of their number is sick, they give him some blessed water and then dance and pray until the patient gets well or dies. Lastly, the greatest number (about two-thirds) are pagans who

126

worship many gods, and have a big shrine to an idol called the "Mother of Kalanama." This juju they believe is capable of giving children to the women of the village. The supernatural powers of witches and wizards have the pagans in awe, and many illnesses which appear incurable are attributed to them.

*August 12*

Another informal discussion was held with the villagers, and we discovered a strange custom among them, namely circumcision of young girls.

This is all part of the marital traditions of the Akugbene people. When a girl reaches womanhood at fifteen years of age, the important event calls for a celebration. People bring money, gifts, and they dance for long hours. The circumcised girl feels happy as she joins the important group beyond puberty. If she does not get circumcised, she will be cursed. The intended husband joins the festival, and it is during the next three or four days that the town finds out whether or not the husband is a responsible person.

When a girl comes of age, she may marry any suitor she chooses. The family holds no sway over her choice, except that interfamily marriage must wait five generations before it is even permitted between cousins. Most marriages are within the Ijaw tribe, but all may marry members of other tribes. However, the non-Ijaw woman must be purchased with a dowry so that the son who may become Père Chief will be "Ijaw purchased" and therefore cannot return to his mother's homeland.

## August 16

Today was the last day of work on the wall. The brick supply has been exhausted, but only the section past the primary school remains to be finished. People in neighboring towns were peeved that we only came to visit, not to set up a Crossroads project; but they understood we had only so much time and people available for the work.

Père Kalanama VI, the Chief of Akugbene, and the townspeople feted us with a banquet at the town meeting hall. Women carried in large bowls of rice and sauce with ram meat, and many speeches were made. The people asked us for autographs and plied us with gifts, and the Chief asked us to realize that the need is great here among the Ijaw. The forests, he said, are rich in wealth, but there are no factories to utilize them and the tribes cannot build them without help.

It was sad leaving Nigeria, but the work we had gotten done, the friends we made and the lessons we've learned are our consolations.

# PART FOUR

---

# ORGANIZATION AND

# ADMINISTRATION

# CHAPTER 1

# CONTROL AND STRUCTURE

What form will the Peace Corps take? Suggestions have run the gamut from wholly private to wholly governmental.

For a time, a decentralized "Peace Corps Foundation" was under serious consideration. It would have been on the model of the National Science Foundation and, like it, administered by a Presidentially appointed board of private citizens. Father Theodore Hesburgh, president of Notre Dame University, and Thomas Melady, a prominent consultant on Africa, were among its principal supporters.

The advantages of this approach are many. Private groups bring to the Government experience and know-how, a self-reliant independence, established procedures and contacts, a notable lack of bureaucratic red tape, and a ready pool of trained technicians. Also, the grass-roots basis of their operations had already won them acceptance in neutral circles not always so friendly to Americans.

However, there are disadvantages as well. The present structure of private programs is inadequate to handle a venture as large as the Peace Corps. The changes necessary in administration and organization might not appeal to them. And, in many cases, groups jealous of their independence would be reluctant to make their goals conform to the needs and purpose of the U. S. Government.

The deciding factors, however, which caused the Administration to veto a private foundation were:

1. It would compete with existing foundations.
2. If sponsored by government and private enterprise alike, it would be resented by agencies wholly dependent on private subscription. The Eisenhower "People-to-People" program failed partly because it alienated private groups in this way.
3. Congress would be reluctant to put money carte blanche into programs she doesn't control.
4. The Constitution specifies that a) the President has full responsibility for the conduct of U. S. foreign policy, and b) a clear line of authority must run from him to those responsible to him. A Peace Corps Foundation would fail on both counts.

The wholly governmental approach, favored by the AFL-CIO and some liberal student groups, was also rejected. It was felt that adding another new bureaucracy would be a sure way to lose the "grass-roots" appeal of the Peace Corps. Besides, there would be no advantage in failing to utilize the parent voluntary agencies, and thus antagonize one of the principal sources of support.

According to the Peace Corps Act sponsored by Senator Humphrey, the agency will have a semi-autonomous role within the State Department. The director will be an Assistant Secretary of State, reporting directly to the Secretary of State. Despite the opposition of ICA Director Henry Labouisse, the Peace Corps will not be merged in the new Agency for International Development, the all-inclusive foreign aid setup planned by President Kennedy. This was a victory for Sargent Shriver and other Peace Corps officials, who agree with Asian and African leaders that its special identity and *esprit de corps* would be lost in a massive bureaucracy. Further, the semi-independence of the Peace Corps lessens the possibility that it will be identified with the Cold War aspects of the Mutual Security Program.

The advantages of the Peace Corps Foundation will be preserved in two ways. As a compromise, an Advisory Council will include representatives of educational institutions, voluntary agencies, farm groups and labor unions. And the effort will be diversified among both government and non-government channels, of which there are five: the voluntary agencies; universities and colleges; United Nations agencies; ICA and other U. S. agencies; and direct Peace Corps units.

## THE CHANNELS OF ACTION

### *The Voluntary Agencies*

Since these groups have many ongoing projects and are already established in many underdeveloped countries, the Peace Corps plans to make contracts with them to carry out projects which it will negotiate for them with foreign government. Another possibility is initiation of projects by the private agencies themselves. For this, they will first submit a prospectus of specific operation, and if the Peace Corps approves, the project will be submitted to the government of the host country to negotiate the details.

In this connection, Sargent Shriver has called upon the business and labor communities to supply Peace Corpsmen. He sees American private enterprise contributing their services in public administration and industrial management as government interns, accountants, administrative assistants, statisticians and clerical personnel. It is a commonplace that the governments, both national and local, in the underdeveloped countries do not have the organizational know-how for the wide range of services they must provide their people. And labor groups can supply such skills as plumbers, electricians, transport workers, and teachers for technical trade schools.

Controversy surrounds the use of religious organizations. Still, the Peace Corps recently contracted with the Heifer Project, an interfaith group, to supply volunteers for work in the West Indies. They will not be preaching religion; their job will be to assist small farm families, develop rural youth clubs, teach home economics, and direct adult education.

The Peace Corps has, however, set down three ironclad rules for participation by religious groups:

1. No proselytizing or missionary work will be allowed on Peace Corps projects.
2. No money will be given if this releases church funds for missionary work.
3. Personnel for Peace Corps projects must be accepted without regard to belief or the lack of it.

The World Council of Churches, a Protestant and Eastern Orthodox association, is wary of relations

with a government agency for two reasons. It is afraid
on the score of constitutional requirement for separa-
tion of church and state as well as for the sake of the
churches themselves. Any possibilities that the separate identities of the churches and the U. S. Government might be confused would have to be scrupu-
lously avoided. On the practical side, this is easy to
understand. In Moslem and Hindu countries, a Christian religious group might run the risk of embarrassing
the Peace Corps, while on the other hand, no church-
man would like being thought of as a part of U. S.
foreign policy.

Gordon Boyce, Peace Corps liaison with the private
agencies, has said that, nevertheless, about half of all
such projects will be contracted with church agencies.

## Colleges and Universities

Since 1938, the State Department has operated a
limited Peace Corps-type program under the International Educational Exchange. As the name suggests,
it has been a two-way venture, making grants to both
American and foreign teachers to teach for a year in
an elementary or secondary school or to lecture at a
university or serve as a consultant abroad. And some
57 universities are now under contract with ICA in
37 countries in educational projects. Recently, Teachers College at Columbia University agreed to supply
more than 150 English teachers for service in East
Africa.

One of the principal uses outside of teaching will
be training, research and project evaluation for the
Peace Corps, and the colleges also have unusual resources for recruiting purposes. Presumably, each

educational institution or regional association will have a section devoted to the Peace Corps.

In the past, three types of contracts with universities existed. The old Technical Co-operation Administration (TCA) used the device of borrowing the services of university personnel for duty overseas, and it was a relatively short-term operation.

The second has been to assign a university to maintain a technical mission as part of a foreign country's over-all program. The faculty selected might operate an agricultural extension service, as in the case of land-grant colleges, or as a teacher training team under the country's Ministry of Education.

The third type is a university-to-university exchange, primarily one in which educational and university administration techniques are supplied.

It might be supposed that university contracts would be the most likely to succeed. However, as Harlan Cleveland noted, the internationalization of colleges has not kept up with the swift pace of world events. Sometimes, contract work has been unsatisfactory because the university accepted it primarily for prestige value, and then put it low on its priority list of jobs to be done. In many other cases, however, it has been the fault of the Government in giving complex foreign affairs work to colleges ill-equipped to handle it.

Several studies have suggested that preparation for Peace Corps work should begin before graduation. Specifically, they recommend special undergraduate courses of intensified language, social science, particular and comparative civilization, and teacher training studies. Georgetown University's School of Foreign Service prepares students for the diplomatic corps, and now American University—also in Washington, D. C.—has set up the widely oriented School of International Service. Both draw extensively on foreign affairs authorities and statesmen to give periodic lectures and even to teach regular courses. Present programs in institutions of this sort could be expanded and geared to Peace Corps needs to provide a ready pool of recruits.

## U. S. Government Agencies

Although ICA experts have departed from their traditional aloof role as advisors and have been drawn into the actual operation of technical assistance, still there is a wide gap between what they can do and the work of their native staff. Often an underdeveloped country is so short on qualified manpower that the ICA advisor-technician does not have a staff of any sort. In his initial report to the President, Sargent Shriver underscored the need for "technician-helpers" to supplement the agencies' operations at the working level. Holland and West Germany have, for several years, supplied "junior experts" to do similar work abroad. One of the areas where they might serve, as Senator Humphrey has pointed out, is with the U. S. Information Agency (USIA) as English teachers and as junior librarians to staff information centers in the less accessible parts of a country. However, it would do well to tread cautiously so far as USIA is concerned; this country has made no bones about the primary mission of USIA as America's propaganda voice, and this is not the proper field for the Peace Corps.

137

## Directly Administered Peace Corps Units

The cautious pioneer report of Professor Max Millikan of M.I.T. urged against direct Peace Corps projects. He and others feared the heavy hand of bureaucracy in government programs, while a critical college professor has commented that the provision is merely a convenient loophole which will later be used as an excuse to turn the entire effort into a wholly government operation. The Peace Corps denies this interpretation and explains that there will be "some projects of a size or complexity or novelty or urgency which cannot be carried out, or carried out well, through any of the above channels." The first project announced by the Peace Corps, road construction in Tanganyika, is apparently of this type. The work will be done by a team of twenty surveyors, four geologists and four civil engineers, and an important side effect will be the training of young Tanganyikans in surveying techniques so that they can take over when the Peace Corps "phases out."

For this type of project, the Peace Corps will do its own recruiting, and training will be contracted to selected universities or other facilities.

## The United Nations

The part that UN agencies will play in future Peace Corps operations will be fully explored in the final chapter.

### COST AND FINANCING

Under the Peace Corps Act of Senator Humphrey, the Director will seek separate legislative authority and appropriations from Congress.

Sargent Shriver has estimated costs as of July, 1961, at less than $2 million—or, as he informed an economy-minded Republican senator, "something less than the cost of one trial firing of an Atlas missile at Cape Canaveral, *one!*" This money was authorized by the President's Executive Order establishing the Peace Corps. Shriver also has estimated that costs for fiscal year 1962–1963 will amount to around $40 million. This is expected to cover all expenses, ranging from volunteers' subsistence allowances to the Director's $20,000-a-year salary, and will provide for 3,000 trainees.

Costs might be reduced, it has been suggested, in several ways. Although not required by the Peace Corps, Tanganyika's Government has volunteered to provide housing, medical care, transportation within the country, and an extra training course. How many other hosts will be so generous is not known, but the pattern will probably vary from country to country. Another way might be the use of so-called "counter-part funds," or soft native currency used by certain countries as payment for U. S. loans or grants. Several American businesses and labor unions have, in addition, offered to undertake training of their personnel as Peace Corpsmen at their own expense; both groups have conducted intern and apprentice training programs which might be expanded and oriented toward Peace Corps needs.

Whatever the costs—and they are small compared to other parts of the total foreign aid program—most experts and voluntary agency workers believe the long-run dividends will make the effort more than worth while.

# CHAPTER 2

# ADMINISTRATION IN THE
# HOST COUNTRY

One of the most important insights the United States
has learned from virtually a generation of overseas
work is that aid should be seen as technical and economic *co-operation, not assistance.* In every instance,
an effort of this nature must be as fully *their* program
as *ours.* It is said that no man worth his salt likes
charity, and it was never more true than in relations
between sovereign nations.

When World War II broke out, the common danger
forced the United States and Latin America to recognize their interdependence. President Roosevelt pro-
claimed his Good Neighbor policy, and Nelson Rockefeller was appointed Co-ordinator of Inter-American
Affairs.

Within a short time, Rockefeller saw that each
country would require a crash program in three basic
areas—health, agriculture, and education. In 1942, he
set up the Institute of Inter-American Affairs (IIAA)
to carry out the project.

The unique contribution of IIAA was the *servicio,*
which is the model for most future Peace Corps

operations overseas. The *servicio* operates as a bi-national commission to insure full co-operation between American technicians and their counterparts in the host country. It is set up as an integral, though semi-autonomous, bureau within the appropriate ministry, depending on the type of project. It has four main objectives:

1. The U. S. mission and the host government participate jointly in development operations. Recruiting of local personnel, program and project planning, financing and purchase of necessary supplies, performance and supervision of the individual projects, informing the public and defending the program against criticism—all are tasks which the American and the native staff members should co-operate in doing.
2. In working shoulder-to-shoulder, day by day with his counterpart, the U. S. technician comes to know and understand the man's customs as well as the problems facing his country.
3. Work habits and job techniques can be exchanged to their best advantage and add to the experience of both the U. S. technician and his counterpart.
4. As a direct result, the two are able to combine their know-how and to accomplish much more than if the close association did not exist. The insight both have gained can ease the task of long-range planning and enable them to take care of emergency situations quickly and efficiently.

The *servicio* may be staffed by U. S. technicians and natives alike, but it should ultimately have only one head. Legally, it must exist as a project agency responsible to the local ministry alone. To make the *servicio* an agency of the American Government would destroy it in the eyes of the people it is supposed to serve.[1]

On the other hand, it is important that the operational freedom of the *servicio* have ironclad guarantees. It must be able to establish its own rules for hiring and firing, its own working procedures and its own fiscal management, independent of those of the parent ministry. The value of this can easily be seen in Latin America, particularly in the not-too-distant past when governments and ministries changed hands on the order of every month or so. If the *servicio* in Peru had not been independent of direct government control, between 1943 and 1954 it would have been at the mercy of twelve different ministers of agriculture![2]

## Who Should Staff the Servicio?

Officers of the *servicio* in past operations have been recruited from the leaders of the U. S. technical mission and from members of the host government, the latter constituting the great bulk of the staff. The Colorado State University study has recommended that, in addition, the staff should also include representatives of nongovernmental professions such as businessmen, educators, trade unionists and voluntary agency workers.

Whether or not the director of the *servicio* should be

[1] Peace Corps Director Sargent Shriver said last May that volunteers will be responsible first to the local ministry and second to Corps directors in the host country.

[2] Philip M. Glick, *The Administration of Technical Assistance: Growth in the Americas* (Chicago: University of Chicago Press, 1957).

an American or a national of the host country depends on two factors: 1) is a competent national available for the job, and 2) will the *servicio*'s freedom of action continue despite the appointment of a national? For the most part, competent nationals have not been available, and consequently the U. S. mission chief serves as director. Some of the voluntary agencies feel that in the initial operations of the Peace Corps, an American director is a must. Part of this feeling stems from the realization that Congress might hesitate to contribute substantial sums to a *servicio* unless an American controls the way the money is spent. *Since the servicio is jointly financed,* with the contribution of the host government usually increasing as the program goes along, it is doubtful that Congress would get its wish regardless of who the director is.

### *"Phase Out"*

At what point does a *servicio* project end and the local ministry take over? This is a very real problem in overseas operations, and many programs make one of two mistakes: either they hold on too long or they let go too soon. The *servicio* itself, being an actual unit in the ministry, is seldom discontinued, but individual projects come and go. Some take longer than others, and so no set timetable exists.

The only reliable rule of thumb is that a project should be transferred to the ministry when it is fully in operation *and* an adequate staff has been given sufficient training to keep the project going and on its toes. It may be necessary to look in from time to time to see that it is actually progressing, but meanwhile the *servicio* should go on to other tasks.

The late Tom Dooley once told of his reaction when

he, too, was suddenly faced with the realization that he was no longer needed:

> We explained that our locals had been well trained and that we hoped they would take over from us. I laughingly explained that I had come to give aid to the Lao and had succeeded in working myself out of a job. The Prince exclaimed, "Good!" When he saw my surprise at this he said, "This is what aid should be, Doctor. It should not make the people more dependent upon the aider, or upon the country from which he has come. Aid should work itself into a position where it abolishes any further need of itself." After thinking about this, I agree.[3]

In countries where a severe shortage of high-level manpower exists or where Peace Corps programs are too small to justify the complex setup of the *servicio*, other instruments should be considered for overseas administration. One device is a "joint fund" to which each government makes contributions. Here the host government exercises control over expenditures, but the U. S. mission has a limited veto as well.

Whatever the instrument to be chosen, it is agreed that the Peace Corps preserve the joint operation necessary for effective co-operation.

[3] Tom Dooley, *The Edge of Tomorrow* (New York: Farrar, Straus, 1958).

# CHAPTER 3

# TERMS OF SERVICE

*Length of Assignment*

There has been a running argument for some time now about how long Peace Corps service should be. Thelma How of the American Friends Service Committee said their experience has shown that a point of "diminishing returns" was reached when youths worked overseas for more than two years. The Near East Foundation, however, contends that anything less than three years would be inadequate, and the initial Humphrey bill of 1960 took the same position and specified that the first year should be taken up with training. The preliminary report of Colorado State University argued for a similar program, but it also stated that the Peace Corps must be flexible enough to permit the inclusion of various short-term projects.

When he introduced the Peace Corps bill last June, Senator Humphrey had modified his earlier stand. Instead of the training period being supplemental to the two years of service, it was all put in one package of enlistment.

A student recently asked Sargent Shriver if it wasn't a little expensive to train new people all the time, and he suggested that the Peace Corps allow volunteers so inclined to re-enlist. Shriver said the idea was already under consideration, but no firm answer could be given for now.

## Salary and Allowances

Peace Corpsmen will accumulate $75 a month payable upon completion of their assignment. In addition, they will be paid $2 a day while in training, and they will be provided a modest subsistence allowance on a level with that of their counterparts in the host country.

While overseas, vounteers will have no diplomatic privileges or immunities, and they will not have any PX privileges, but housing, food, medical care and insurance will be covered by their allowance. Disabilities suffered while on Peace Corps duty will entitle volunteers to post-service care and compensation.

Peace Corps leaders, according to the new Humphrey bill, will receive higher allowances and readjustment bonuses. They will also be allowed to bring their wives and children with them, and these dependents will enjoy rights similar to those of U. S. servicemen.

## The Draft

When President Kennedy first proposed the Peace Corps, he suggested it as an alternative to military service. The storm of protest aroused both at home and abroad caused him to drop it like a hot potato, however. An African newspaper observed that if the Peace Corps was worth a draft exemption, then it must be tied in with America's mutual security or military defense effort. Lewis Carliner of the United

Auto Workers disputed the "draft-dodging" theory, and said that many students could not afford three years in the Peace Corps and still be subject to two years in uniform.

The furor quieted down a bit when General Lewis Hershey, Director of the Selective Service, pointed out that service with the Peace Corps would entitle volunteers to deferment. When they returned, they would probably continue to be deferred because of age and useful employment.

## What Happens When the Peace Corpsman Returns Home?

When his enlistment is up, the Peace Corpsman will receive his bonus to tide him over until he finds a job. The Peace Corps has set up a career-planning board to seek out prospective employers and explain to them the nature of the volunteer's experience and performance overseas.

Some have suggested that the Government adopt the program used by Standard Oil of New Jersey. When one of their men is abroad for a long time, he is paid local salary rates. When he returns home after two to six years' absence, the company credits him with seniority for the time spent overseas, and his full American salary for the entire period is given to him.

However, the primary hope of Administration officials is that former Peace Corpsmen will enter U. S. Government or international service. Some could rejoin the Peace Corps, but this time as instructors in training or as field leaders. The over-all effect of the "grass-roots" co-operation program, it is hoped, will be to widen American experience in international affairs from Oshkosh to Montgomery.

147

# PART FIVE

AN INTERNATIONAL
PEACE CORPS?

Last April, U. S. Ambassador Adlai Stevenson urged the United Nations to take the American Peace Corps under it wing, and the proposal was warmly received by the Afro-Asian neutralist bloc.

Is an International Peace Corps feasible? Eighty per cent of the private voluntary agencies, with years of sober experience, advise the Peace Corps to go slow. The new agency should get its feet firmly on the ground and a few pilot projects underway before it starts expanding in any direction, they say.

Another line of thought disagrees with the private agencies. The size of any technical co-operation mission, they argue, depends on five factors: the availability of qualified volunteers, leaders, suitable projects, training staff and facilities, and, last but not least, money. The United States cannot supply all these resources, but an international body could.

But can the United Nations do it? The UN Expanded Program of Technical Assistance has been declining in scope and importance in comparison with nation-to-nation and regional aid programs. At its best, UNEPTA has never been able to raise in voluntary subscription more than $34 million—and the United States furnished roughly half of this sum. The UN has adequate machinery to set up an International Peace Corps, but it never seems to be able to come up with the necessary money.

Some argue that an International Peace Corps would strengthen the UN and its specialized agencies. But how true is this? The United States could unilaterally finance the new body, but wouldn't this actually work to compromise the UN? During the Congo crisis, the air was filled with neutralist accusations that the UN had become a puppet of the United States and her NATO allies.

On a point of procedure, multilateral agreements of the kind that would have to be negotiated under the UN are more painful than pulling a tooth. The 99-plus interests represented in the UN General Assembly must all be pacified, and often the resultant compromise is almost unrecognizable. The American Peace Corps requires only a nation-to-nation negotiation, and even its agreements will have to undergo considerable revision before they are finally put into effect.

But the problems of the underdeveloped areas are so immense that the United States can alleviate but a small part. If India, for example, wants to raise her daily diet by as little as 100 calories—or the equivalent of a single slice of bread—she must have over 5 million more tons of food grains each year. The problem has caused strong men to flinch. Norman Cousins tells of such a man, a young American who quit India after only five months' service. "It's no use," he said. "You help one man only to discover fifty men standing behind him. Then you help fifty men and five thousand suddenly appear. You help the five thousand but what do you do about the five million behind them and the fifty million to follow? At some point along the line you decide it's hopeless." [1]

Somebody has to do it, though. The rest of the world, the prosperous Western nations, can't just stand by and watch as the gap between the rising expectations and the insufficient resources of the underdeveloped nations widens. But for human misery, Western Europe need look no farther than its own backyard. In Sicily, home of the Mafia, unemployment and poverty run rampant, and half the available labor force of Palermo alone is without jobs and adequate food and clothes.

Many of the medium skills that are needed could be provided by the U. S. Peace Corps—but there aren't that many personnel available in the United States.

What then can be done? For one, UN member states could loan junior technicians to projects of the specialized agencies, especially the International Labor Organization, the World Health Organization and UNESCO.

Ambassador Stevenson suggested that nations providing volunteers should assume all maintenance allowances, insurance and transportation costs, while, as in the Tanganyika project, the countries receiving UNEPTA aid could help with local expenses.

"Expenses for the central administration," he said further, ". . . should as far as possible be a charge of the regularly assessed budgets of the UN."

Another way to reduce unilateralism would be to send out international teams in co-operation with such

[1] "Confrontation," *Saturday Review*, March 25, 1961.

regional groups as the Organization of American States and with private foreign enterprises like the British Voluntary Services Overseas and the German Council for Development Aid.

The need for a peace corps has been established. These are but a few of the ways in which it can be used. Probably it will not be too long before some sort of international peace corps will be set up under the auspices of the United Nations, despite the difficulties involved.

If the Peace Corps is well managed and executed with caution and tact every step of the way, then it will live up to its name and make a contribution similar to the Marshall Plan which rejuvenated Europe. If it is mishandled and loses the hardheaded sense of practical idealism now behind it, then it may well be one of the greatest fiascos in history.